DB2 SQL 75+ Tuning Tips
For Developers

DB2 SQL 75+ Tuning Tips
For Developers

By

Tony Andrews
Application Tuning Consultant
P+T Solutions, Inc.
www.pandtsolutions.com

AKA 'Tony the Tuner'

I can tune a query but I can't tuna fish

www.db2sqltuningtips.com

©P+T Solutions, Inc.

Copyright and Trademark Notice

To Order more books, visit www.db2sqltuningtips.com

TABLE OF CONTENTS

FORWARD, DEDICATION, DISCLAIMER

CHAPTER 1:   SQL OPTIMIZATION TOP 75+

CHAPTER 2:   DB2 SQL HINTS

CHAPTER 3:   SQL STANDARDS AND GUIDELINES

CHAPTER 4:   SQL PROGRAM WALKTHROUGHS

CHAPTER 5:   EXISTENCE CHECKING

CHAPTER 6:   RUNSTATS

CHAPTER 7:   TEN STEPS TO TUNING A QUERY

APPENDIX A: PREDICATE REWRITE EXAMPLES

APPENDIX B: DB2 SQL TERMINOLOGY

FORWARD

Most relational tuning experts agree that the majority of performance problems among applications that access a relational database are caused by poorly coded programs or improperly coded SQL. Industry experts also note that poor performing SQL is responsible for as much as 80 percent of response-time issues. I personally agree with this. Of all the IT shops for which I have provided performance and tuning consulting work in, most of the performance issues are directly related to modifying application and SQL code, or adding and altering indexes. That is why I continually try to educate developers in the ways of SQL programming and associated performance issues. I also believe more developers should be educated in how to read and analyze DB2 Explain output. In addition I believe that every large development project involved with a RDMS should have an SQL technical expert as part of the project. There are many SQL developers in the IT industry, but based on my experience, I have found that less than 10% of them really know the performance issues involved with SQL programming or how to fix them. By having an SQL technical expert, many performance and logic issues can be caught before ever migrating to production.

The purpose of this book is to provide a reference for developers who need to tune an SQL statement or program. Most developers are too quick to blame the network, the database, the system, the high volume of transactions, etc., for the slowness of their program or application. Yet most of the time the slowness is directly related to their code. Hopefully, this book will give them something to fall back on before calling DBAs or others, and try first to improve the performance issue(s) at hand.

There are also times when SQL, along with the Explain, looks good, but is not performing efficiently. This book also provides some 'Tuning Tips' to tweak the SQL into possibly optimizing differently than the optimizer had chosen. These are tips that many experts in the industry use to get poor performing SQL statements to optimize differently and possibly execute faster, especially when time is an issue in getting performance issues fixed.

I have included a list of SQL Standards and Guidelines that I have implemented in numerous shops. If there are no SQL standards set up in your IT shop, then these would be a great place to start. Many shops choose to add more items to the list specific to their applications.

It's one thing to have in place Standards and Guidelines, and then it's another to ensure they are followed. I have been in many shops where they show me their shop standards for SQL programming, Cobol programming, Java programming, etc., but have no quality assurance set up to ensure that the standards are being followed. All programs going into production should have some kind of code walkthrough or review to ensure standards are followed, and also to ensure that their SQL was correctly written. The reviews are also a way to ensure that program and SQL logic is correct and the design of the program fits its needs. There is a chapter of items that should be asked and checked when performing code walkthroughs involving SQL programming. The minimal amount of time for a code walkthrough far offsets any production performance or logic issues that may arise.

Many times developers have SQL code to tune and are not sure where to start. The first place I tell them is to look at all the predicates in each query and try to write them more efficient if possible. This book provides an appendix of poor performing SQL predicates and a more efficient way to rewrite them. It is important for developers whether a predicate is indexable or non indexable, and whether a predicate Stage 1 or Stage 2. These are discussed in more detail later in this book.

Performance is not so much a DB2 issue as it is a relational issue. Developers have to be careful how they structure the queries, and how they design their application code around the queries. Database analysts and database modelers have to be careful how they design a database application. They need to take their time and do a good analysis. Performance depends on environment, applications and requirements. And performance, no matter how good it is, can always be better. Although the majority of tuning efforts are spent at the operating system and database level, the largest performance gains are obtained from tuning the application code. Applications that use SQL to retrieve data in a database are the best candidates for tuning. Since a relatively small number of SQL statements consume the majority of resources, SQL tuning often results in significant performance improvements. However, SQL tuning can at times be complex. This book provides a place to start and tries to keep simple the things that developers can do in order to get SQL driven programs and applications to perform more efficiently.

DISCLAIMER

"The tuning tips and comments in this book are my own personal opinions based on many years of designing, programming, and tuning DB2 applications. Some of the tuning tips may not necessarily reflect the positions or opinions of IBM, any of their affiliates, or so called experts in the field. These tuning tips are based upon my personal experience and have all been used from time to time in applications I have been a part of to obtain better performance. I have personally used each of the 75+ tips when tuning DB2 SQL applications in order to get queries and programs to execute more efficiently.

Everyone knows the saying 'It Depends'. Please keep this in mind. Do not take every tip in this book and automatically expect instant performance gains. The tips are intended to give developers some direction and ideas to improve their queries or programs. Everyone should always conduct their own independent tests to verify the validity of any statements made in this book before automatically basing decisions upon those statements."

Thank You,

Tony Andrews AKA
'Tony the Tuner'

DEDICATION

This book is dedicated to the many DB2 SQL professional developers who want to do the best they can, but are not sure where to start when performance is an issue. It is also for those that do not have the time or resources to improve their skills. I have worked with so many developers over the years and am continually impressed by their commitment and abilities to getting the jobs done, and the commitment to their profession. But I have also noticed that when it comes to performance and tuning of SQL statements, programs, or applications, that most are unsure of what exactly to do. Performance and tuning at times can be quite obvious and easy, and other times can be quite involved. My hope is that this book will help educate those in these areas and provide for them a place to go for answers and direction.

CHAPTER 1: SQL OPTIMIZATION TOP 75+

The following are some of the most effective things developers can do in their SQL code to ensure better performance. 90% of the runtime problems in a RDMS come from 10% of application issues. Today's DB2 optimizer is better than ever in selecting the correct access paths to fulfill SQL requests, but it can never be 100% correct. All tuning efforts are directly related to CPU usage, I/O, and concurrency. Most of the topics in this chapter are specific to SQL coding, but all topics are related to performance and tuning.

Poorly coded programs or improperly coded SQL statements are most often the culprit causing poor performance. The SQL language seems quite easy to learn and master, but there are many inefficiencies in how the DB2 optimizer handles the language when it comes to performance. Developers, testers, DBAs, and business analysts alike will all benefit from this book providing them with many tips specific to coding proper SQL for efficiency.

The book's focus is to increase developers' knowledge in the ways of performance and tuning in an IBM DB2 relational database environment. In an organized and easy-to-understand format, it provides development tips, suggestions, and many SQL coding examples, all with the purpose of gaining better performance.

All of the SQL coding examples reference the DB2 sample tables found in every DB2 site, and noted throughout all of the IBM DB2 manuals.

1) Take out any / all Scalar functions coded on columns in predicates.

There is usually a way to recode the predicate without using a function on a column. Remember: Scalar functions are perfectly fine when placed on columns in the Select portion of the SQL statement, but will automatically make a predicate non-indexable if used on columns in the Where portion. For example:

> SELECT EMPNO, LASTNAME
> FROM EMPLOYEE
> WHERE YEAR(HIREDATE) = 2005

Should be coded as:

> SELECT EMPNO, LASTNAME
> FROM EMPLOYEE
> WHERE HIREDATE BETWEEN '2005-01-01'
>   and '2005-12-31'

By rewriting this statement, DB2 may now choose to use an index on the column HIREDATE if one exists. Having it coded with the YEAR function in the predicate will not allow DB2 to use an index.

2) Take out any / all mathematics coded on columns in predicates.

There is usually a way to recode the predicate without using mathematics on a column. Using mathematics is perfectly fine when placed on columns in the Select portion of the SQL statement, but will automatically make a predicate non-indexable if used on columns in the Where portion. For example:

```
SELECT EMPNO, LASTNAME
FROM EMPLOYEE
WHERE SALARY * 1.1 > 50000.00
```

Should be coded as:

```
SELECT EMPNO, LASTNAME
FROM EMPLOYEE
WHERE SALARY > 50000.00 / 1.1
```

By rewriting this statement, DB2 may now choose to use an index on the column SALARY if one exists. Having it coded with mathematics directly applied to the SALARY column will not allow DB2 to use an index. Always have columns coded by themselves on one side of the operator, and all calculations on the opposite side.

3) Only code the columns needed in the Select portion of the SQL statement.

By having columns that are not needed, the optimizer may choose Indexonly = 'N' which forces DB2 to also go to the datapage in order to get specific columns requested, requiring more I/O. It can also make sorting more expensive due to extra columns that may be part of any sorts, which causes a larger sort file to be created. Size has a direct cost associated with sorts. They are as expensive as their size.

Having extra columns specified can also have an effect on the optimizer's choice of join type if there are multiple tables in the query. Currently there are 4 types of joins in Z/OS DB2 (Nested Loop, Merge Scan, Hybrid, and Star), along with the Hash join in DB2 UDB. Each has their reasons for being chosen by the optimizer. Having extra columns that are not used may keep the optimizer from making the best choice in join processing.

4) Stay away from 'Distinct' if at all possible.

Most of the time, the Distinct function causes a sort of the final result set, making it one of the more expensive sorts. This has always been one the most expensive functions in the SQL language. There are changes as of DB2 V9 where the optimizer will look to take advantage of an index to eliminate a sort for uniqueness as it currently does in optimizing with a 'Group By' statement. Anytime a query can be rewritten to obtain the same results without having the 'Distinct' in the SQL is most of the time more efficient. Developers today are very 'Distinct' happy, with many coding it on all on statements to ensure no duplicates show up. This is not inefficient coding. One of the first things I always do when tuning applications is to scan source code and grab all the statements containing 'Distinct', understand if the query really gets duplicates, and rewrite them. With a thorough analysis of nightly batch jobs, this can easily knock time off the batch cycles.

If duplicates are to be eliminated from the result set, try:

- 'Group By' which looks to take advantage of any
  associated indexes to eliminate a sort for uniqueness.
- Rewriting the query using an 'In' or 'Exists' subquery.
  This will work if the table causing the duplicates (due to a
  one to many relationship) does not have data being
  returned as part of the result set.

continued…

'Distinct' cont...

For Example: Provide a list of employees that are currently working on projects. Many of the employees work on multiple projects at the same time, but we only want to see them once.

```
SELECT DISTINCT E.EMPNO, E.LASTNAME
FROM EMPLOYEE      E,
      EMPPROJACT  EP
WHERE E.EMPNO = EP.EMPNO
```

Can also be rewritten as:

```
SELECT E.EMPNO, E.LASTNAME
FROM EMPLOYEE      E,
      EMPPROJACT  EP
WHERE E.EMPNO = EP.EMPNO
 GROUP BY E.EMPNO, E.LASTNAME
```

Can also be rewritten as:

```
SELECT E.EMPNO, E.LASTNAME
 FROM EMPLOYEE  E
 WHERE EXISTS
     (SELECT 1
      FROM  EMPPROJACT  EP
      WHERE E.EMPNO = EP.EMPNO)
```

Can also be rewritten as:

```
SELECT E.EMPNO, E.LASTNAME
FROM EMPLOYEE  E
WHERE E.EMPNO IN
     (SELECT EP.EMPNO
      FROM  EMPPROJACT  EP)
```

5) Try rewriting an 'In' subquery as an 'Exists' subquery.

Each of these will produce the same results, but operate very differently. Typically one will perform better than the other depending on data distributions. For Example:

```
SELECT E.EMPNO, E.LASTNAME
FROM EMPLOYEE E
WHERE E.EMPNO IN
    (SELECT D.MGRNO
      FROM DEPARTMENT D
      WHERE D.DEPTNO LIKE 'D%")
```

Can also be coded as:

```
SELECT E.EMPNO, E.LASTNAME
FROM EMPLOYEE E
WHERE EXISTS
    (SELECT 1
      FROM DEPARTMENT D
      WHERE D.MGRNO = E.EMPNO
          AND D.DEPTNO LIKE 'D%')
```

6) Always make sure Host Variables are defined to match the column's datatype.

This is especially important for Cobol programmers. If a column is defined as a small integer, than the host variable that it is being compared to must be of the same definition, like S9(4) comp for Cobol. This has been improved as of DB2 V8 where it handles different numeric datatypes and different character strings being compared more efficiently. Some development languages do not have all the same datatypes as can be defined in DB2 which caused problems in the past. But as a general rule, making the declared datatypes match the column definition ensures the most efficient performance and optimization. For example if a column is defined as an integer datatype, than any host variable containing values for comparison in a predicate should have an integer definition (not smallint, decimal, floating point, etc.). This could make the predicate non-indexable.

Another example is one which a string column is being compared to a string of larger length, making the predicate non-indexable. For Example:

SELECT E.EMPNO, E.LASTNAME
FROM EMPLOYEE E
WHERE DEPTNO = 'A00   '

DEPTNO is a column defined as character 3, being compared against a character 6 hard coded variable. This makes the predicate non-indexable. But if the hard coded variable is a length less than the definition, then that is indexable. DB2 V8 nows has this predicate with longer character strings as Stage 1, but it is still not indexable.

Cobol programmers should always use the created DCLGEN host variables to ensure exact matches.

7) Avoid 'Or' in predicates as much as possible, especially when they are within a predicate enclosed in parenthesis.

Split the predicates out if possible. The following example will clarify this better. The idea here is to get the 'OR' out from *within* the parenthesis, and move it *outside* the parenthesis. Many times this will move the optimizer to indexable from non indexable, or possibly move the optimizer to choose a multi index processing access path. For Example:

```
SELECT DEPTNO, DEPTNAME
FROM DEPARTMENT
WHERE (ADMRDEPT = 'E01' OR
        DEPTNO = 'D01')
    AND  DEPTNAME LIKE 'BRANCH%'
```

Should be recoded as:

```
SELECT DEPTNO, DEPTNAME
FROM DEPARTMENT
WHERE (ADMRDEPT  = 'E01'
        AND DEPTNAME LIKE 'BRANCH%')
   OR (ADMRDEPT = 'D01'
        AND DEPTNAME LIKE 'BRANCH%')
```

8) Make sure the data distribution statistics are current in the tables being processed.

This is done by executing the Runstats utility on each specific table and associated indexes. This utility loads up the system catalog tables with data distribution information that the optimizer looks for when selecting access paths. Some of the information that the Runstats utility provides:

- The size of the table (number of rows)
- The cardinalities of the index columns
- The frequency of rows by values for certain columns
- The physical characteristics of the table files
- Information by partition for partition tables
- Etc...

If table statistics are not loaded, or if table statistics are out of date, then the optimizer may choose access paths that are not specifically suited to the tables. This may hinder performance. For example if a table contains 5 million rows, but the last Runstats took place when the table contained 200,000 rows, then DB2 still thinks it is a rather small table, and knows nothing about 5 million rows.

In the system catalog tables, there is a column named STATSTIME that gives the exact date and time of the last Runstats for that table. If this column contains the value '0001-01-01-00.00.00.000000', then either no Runstats process has been executed on the table, or Runstats information has been reset. For DB2 UDB the STATSTIME is null if no Runstats has been run.

See chapter 6 on Runstats processing.

continued...

Data distribution statistics cont...

The system catalog tables updated by Runstats, and viewed by the optimizer are:

- SYSIBM.SYSCOLDIST
- SYSIBM.SYSCOLDISTSTATS
- SYSIBM.SYSCOLSTATS
- SYSIBM.SYSCOLUMNS
- SYSIBM.SYSINDEXES
- SYSIBM.SYSINDEXPART
- SYSIBM.SYSINDEXSTATS
- SYSIBM.SYSTABLES
- SYSIBM.SYSTABLEPART
- SYSIBM.SYSTABLESPACE
- SYSIBM.SYSTABSTATS

See the System Catalog section for more information on Catalog Tables.

9) Make sure of 'Union' versus 'Union All'.

Most developers automatically code 'Union' when needed, which always causes a sort to take place to eliminate any duplicates. Many times duplicates will never exist between the separate queries, so the SQL statement should be coded as 'Union All', which will then eliminate a useless sort.

For example:

```
SELECT DEPTNO
 FROM DEPARTMENT
 WHERE MGRNO in ('000010', '000020', '000030')
UNION
 SELECT DEPTNO
 FROM PROJECT
 WHERE PROJNO = 'PA1000'
```

By having the 'UNION' statement, DB2 will automatically execute a final sort to eliminate any DEPTNO duplicates. But there are many queries like this where there may never be any duplicates between the queries. And in those cases, if UNION is coded, DB2 will still execute a useless sort looking for duplicates.

Also, developers often times code the UNION as a safety net just in case duplicates show. This is not a good coding practice. Developers should know their data and relationships well enough to know for sure if duplicates could ever occur. This same topic also holds true when coding DISTINCT.

10) Consider hard coding versus a host variable.

This is especially important for Cobol programmers where they use Host Variable working storage fields within their SQL statements. Most Cobol programs are written as Static SQL programs, not Dynamic SQL programs. For these Cobol programs, when the DB2 Bind gets executed against the program, the optimizer does not know the actual values that will be in the working storage host variables until runtime. So when the optimizer is choosing access paths for an SQL statement, it has some default rules that it goes by. For example:

There exists a table with 1 million rows. In this table exists an index on the column Status_Code. After a typical Runstats utility is executed against this table, the optimizer will know that there are 3 different values for the status code. After a special Runstats that specifies frequency value statistics for that column, DB2 will know the following data distributions:

- Status Code value 'A' contains 50% of the data
- Status Code value 'B' contains 45% of the data
- Status Code value 'C' contains 05% of the data.

The Cobol program contains the following SQL. The value is always 'C' that comes into the program:

```
SELECT COL1, COL2, COL3
FROM TABLE
WHERE STATUS_CD = :WS-STATUS_CD
```

continued…

Consider hard coding versus a Host Variable cont…

When the optimizer at bind time is figuring out an access path using a host variable, it does not know what value is to be processed, but it does know there are 3 different values across 1 million rows. Its default rule is that it thinks no matter what the value is at runtime, approximately 1/3 of the data will be retrieved. Thinking that 1/3 of the data is to be retrieved, many times it will choose a tablespace scan of the data.

If the Cobol program contains the following SQL:

```
SELECT COL1, COL2, COL3
 FROM TABLE
 WHERE STATUS_CD = 'C'
```

now the optimizer with the hardcoded 'C' can further look through the system catalog tables, and see that only 05% of the data has the value 'C' for the STATUS_CODE column, and because of this chooses to use the index for its access path choice.

To always hardcode values in code is not the standard or even a guideline for coding practices in SQL. But there are many times when hard coding a value can drastically change the access path chosen, providing much better performance. This is especially true when there exist some values for columns that have very skewed data distributions. Keep in mind that a special Runstats typically needs to run in order to get the extra distribution statistics. These are called frequency value statistics.

11) Minimize the SQL requests to DB2.

This is huge in performance tuning of programs, especially batch programs because they tend to process more data. Every time an SQL call is sent to the database manager, there is overhead in sending the SQL statement to DB2, going from one address space in the operating system to another address space for DB2 execution. So in general developers need to minimize:

- The number of time cursors are Opened/Closed
- The number of random SQL requests (noted as synchronized reads in DB2 monitors).

Many developers think and code very procedurally. When developing with Relational Database Management Systems and coding in SQL, developers need to think more relationally. That is, they need to think 'How can I get everything I need by sending the minimal number of SQL statements to the database manager, instead of making so many procedural calls?' Even though a single Select statement may be extremely efficient for DB2 to execute, there is overhead incurred in just sending the statement to DB2.

Now there is a balance between trying to put everything into one cursor and being able to maintain and understand the logic. But just remember that if you can cut down 10% or more of the calls to DB2 out of a program, that program will most definitely run faster.

continued...

Minimize the SQL requests to DB2 cont...

Following these guidelines will help:

- Code a multi table join instead of breaking it up into separate cursors. Do not code with the style of having a 'Driver Cursor', then as rows are fetched, branch off and open/close other cursors. Instead, code it all in one statement.
- Code Outer joins instead of randomly executing existence checking, then check for nulls from a column in the other table to know whether there was existence or not.
- Code an Exists Subbquery instead of randomly executing separate existence checking queries to get back only those rows that exists.
- Get columns formatted in the Select as needed, and do not execute other SQL statements to do so. Apply whatever SQL scalar functions are needed on a column in the Select portion of the SQL statement in order to mask it exactly as needed.
- Get all dates needed in one statement instead of sending separate statements.

For Example:

```
SELECT CURRENT DATE + 7 DAYS,
       CURRENT DATE – 7 DAYS,
       LAST_DAY(CURRENT DATE)
FROM SYSIBM.SYSDUMMY1
```

12) Try rewriting 'Range' predicates as 'Between' predicates.

Suppose a query is not performing well and one of the main filtering predicates is a range predicate, such as:

WHERE HIREDATE > :HV-DATE

If the database manager has not chosen to use the index on HIREDATE, and you want to try and get it to move to that index, then try coding the following:

WHERE HIREDATE BETWEEN
            :HV-DATE and :HV-DATE2

Just make sure the 2nd variable is set to some extreme and is contained in a host variable field (in this case '9999-12-31'). Note that this will only work with host variables. The optimizer is smart enough to know that a hard coded '9999-12-31' really does not change the logic. But if it sees a variable, it does not know the value until runtime, whereas it optimizes (or prepares) before the value gets set. So the optimizer is really being fooled to think that the 'Between' predicate is going to filter more than it actually is.

This is not a guarantee, but the optimizer does look at between predicates much different than range predicates and calculates the predicate's filter factor differently. But it gives developers something to try, and many time will change the optimization path.

continued…

Rewrite 'Range' predicates as 'Between' cont...

Note: This will not work if the SQL is coming from a dynamic statement, but only for those programs coming from a static SQL statement (like Cobol binds or JAVA prepares) where DB2 does not know what values are in the host variables until execution.

If someone changes the code from:

WHERE HIREDATE > ? to

WHERE HIREDATE BETWEEN ? and '9999-12-31'

there will be no change in the access path chosen because with hard coded variables, DB2 knows that what is coded is a maximum value and will optimize based on that value. It will be no different to DB2 than the range predicate.

Remember: DB2 can figure out a lot more if the variables are hard coded than if they're not. Sometimes hard coding can be good for access path choices; other times it will not help at all. But with very skewed data as in this example, hard coding is what the optimizer needs.

13) Consider the use of Global Temporary Tables.

Consider Global Temporary tables if the data being processed will persist within the application's logical unit of work, rather than repeated constitution or materialization of data. If the same data is being retrieved or materialized multiple times throughout a program's execution, then load the data one time into a Global Temporary Table, and reference that table elsewhere in the code.

For Example: A program has multiple cursors, and each cursor contains multiple table joins. Also, each cursor contains the same table 'Table1' that happens to be the driver table in each query. As each cursor gets processed, the same rows may have to be retrieved from the database for processing on Table1. This causes extra I/O against the same data.

So the idea is to retrieve only Table1 data and insert it into a Global Temporary Table, then reference the Global table in each cursor. This eliminates the duplicate I/O on Table1.

Warning: There are two types of Global Temporary Tables, those that are Created by the DBAs, and those that are Declared within application code. Be careful when using the global tables created by the DBAs because they can not have indexes. When these are part of a multi table join, it could cause performance issues. But when a global table is declared within application code, an index can be created on the table in the application code before loading data into it. When this occurs, dynamic statistics are gathered as data gets inserted, and it typically becomes more efficient in joins because of its index and statistics.

continued…

Global Temporary Tables cont...

Following is an example of declaring and creating a GTT in code. When declaring these in application code, the owner must = SESSION.

```
DECLARE GLOBAL TEMPORARY TABLE
                            SESSION.TEMP_EMP
 (EMPNO      CHAR(6)       NOT NULL,
  FIRSTNME   VARCHAR(12)  NOT NULL,
  MIDINIT    CHAR(1)       NOT NULL,
  LASTNAME   VARCHAR(15)  NOT NULL,
  WORKDEPT   CHAR(3),
  PHONENO    CHAR(4)
 )
;

CREATE INDEX SESSION.EMPX1 ON SESSION.TEMP_EMP
   (LASTNAME  ASC)

;

INSERT INTO SESSION.TEMP_EMP
 SELECT EMPNO,
       FIRSTNME,
       MIDINIT,
       LASTNAME,
       DEPTNO,
       PHONENO
 FROM EMP
;
```

continued...

Global Temporary Tables cont...

```
 SELECT *
FROM SESSION.TEMP_EMP
 ;
```

Note: Your DBAs may want you to add some of the following to the create statements. Make sure to consult them before coding up in your program.
--
-- USING STOGROUP SYSDEFLT (OR SOME OTHER)
-- PRIQTY 999 - PRIMARY DATAFILE SIZE
-- SECQTY 999 - SECONDARY DATAFILE SIZE
-- BUFFERPOOL BXX - ASSIGNED BUFFERPOOL

14) Give prominence to Stage 1 over Stage 2 Predicates.

To retrieve data, DB2 uses a two-stage architecture. The Data Manager, called Stage 1, has traditionally applied simple SQL predicates and can use indexes to retrieve the data. Sometimes, Stage 1 predicates are called "sargable" (an IBM term meaning searchargumentable or searchableargument). If the Data Manager can't handle the predicate, it's passed to the Relational Data Services (RDS) part of DB2 as a Stage 2 (residual) predicate.

Stage 1 predicates are better for performance than Stage 2 because the passage of data between the stages takes place at the column-value level. If rows are qualified at Stage 1, fewer rows will have to be passed to Stage 2. Indexes can further narrow the search and reduce processing. Making sure SQL queries request only the columns that are actually needed can also limit the amount of processing needed to return an answer set.

Always try to code predicates as Stage 1 and indexable. In general, Stage 2 predicates do not perform as well and consume extra CPU. See the IBM SQL Reference Guide to determine what predicates are Stage 1 vs. Stage 2 and make sure to go to the correct Version of DB2 when checking. Each new release typically changes many Stage 2 predicates to Stage 1 predicates for better efficiency. Some DB2 Explain tools will split out the predicates in each SQL statement into the Stage 1 predicates and Stage 2 predicates.

continued…

Give prominence to Stage 1 cont...

Non indexable predicates are those predicates that by definition the way they are coded will not allow DB2 to process using an index on the column involved. Stage 2 predicates are those that always get applied after data retrieval versus during data retrieval. Typically stage 2 predicates can be rewritten differently, making them stage 1.

The current version (V8) of the Visual Explain tool does break out all predicates in a query into different categories of Matching Index, Screening Index, Stage 1, and Stage 2. This is a great tool to get a quick visual to see if any stage 2 predicates exist that should be looked at and rewritten.

See Appendix A Predicate Rewrites. Also see stage 1 and stage 2 definitions in the terminology chapter.

The following link will take you to the current V8 of the IBM manuals. Search on 'stage 1'.

http://www-306.ibm.com/software/data/db2/zos/v8books.html

15) Order of Predicates Does Matter (Some)

Code your predicates starting with the most restrictive to least restrictive by table, by predicate type. When writing a SQL statement with multiple predicates, write the predicate that will filter out the most data from the result set as the first predicate. By sequencing the predicates from most restrictive to least restrictive, all subsequent predicates have less data to filter.

The DB2 optimizer by default will pick and choose which predicates it wants to process first by certain predicate categories. However, if the query presents multiple predicates that fall into the same category, these predicates will be executed in the order that they are written. This is why it is important to sequence the predicates, placing the predicates with the most filtering at the top of the predicate list.

This is not a tuning tip that will help a query go from hours to minutes, or minutes to seconds, but when tuning any SQL statements, every little bit helps.

16). Streamline Multiple Subqueries:

Many times an SQL statement will contain multiple subqueries, and DB2 has it rules on how it will process them.

1) When the subqueries are either all Correlated or all Non Correlated, then physically code them in the order of most restrictive first.
2) If an SQL statement contains both Correlated and Non Correlated subqueries, the Non Correlated subqueries will always be executed first, not matter the physical ordering in the query.
3) As a developer, we have the option to code the subqueries all the same type, and physically order them in the predicate list as we choose, which at times can make a difference in runtime. Coding subqueries from most restrictive to least restrictive in an SQL statement has a much bigger impact on performance than regular predicates as stated in tuning tip #15.

Example of a Non Correlated subquery:

```
SELECT E.EMPNO, E.LASTNAME
FROM EMPLOYEE E
WHERE E.EMPNO IN
    (SELECT D.MGRNO
     FROM DEPARTMENT D
     WHERE D.DEPTNO LIKE 'D%")
```

Example of a Correlated subquery:

```
SELECT E.EMPNO, E.LASTNAME
FROM EMPLOYEE E
WHERE EXISTS
    (SELECT 1
     FROM DEPARTMENT D
     WHERE D.MGRNO = E.EMPNO
       AND D.DEPTNO LIKE 'D%')
```

17) Index Correlated Subqueries:

There are a couple of things to pay attention to when an SQL statement is processing using a Correlated subquery.

- Correlated subqueries can get executed many times in order to fulfill the SQL request. With this in mind, the subquery must be processed using an index to alleviate multiple tablespace scans.
- If the correlated subquery is getting executed hundreds of thousands or millions of times, then it is best to make sure the subquery gets executed using an index with Indexonly = Yes. This may require an index change or the altering of an already existing index.

For example:

```
SELECT E.EMPNO, E.LASTNAME
FROM EMPLOYEE E
WHERE EXISTS
      (SELECT 1
       FROM DEPARTMENT D
       WHERE D.MGRNO = E.EMPNO
         AND D.DEPTNO LIKE 'D%')
```

In this example, the subquery will get executed 32 times because that is how many different EMPNOs will get passed to the subquery. The subquery will use an index (MGRNO Index), but then has to go to the table's data file to check for the predicate A.DEPTNO LIKE 'D%'.

continued…

Index Correlated Subqueries cont...

So every time the subquery gets executed, two I/Os are taking place. One for the index file, and then another for the table's data file. This subquery only getting executed 32 times will not have much effect, but if the outer query feeds millions of values to the subquery, then the extra I/O adds up dramatically. In those cases, I would recommend an index that contains both columns (MGRNO, DEPTNO) which would then eliminate the 2nd I/O to the data file, and the DB2 Explain would show the optimization as Indexonly = Yes for the subquery processing.

For subqueries that are executed millions of times, this will have a huge effect on runtime.

18) Get to know your DB2 Explain tool:

Every DB2 SQL developer should know how to analyze the information that comes out when executing a DB2 Explain against a query. This is an extremely useful tool stating which access path the optimizer has chosen for a specific query. There are various Explain tools on the market, and every DB2 shop has the ability to execute explains. So become familiar with whatever tool is used at your shop to execute an Explain. The DB2 Explain will answer some of the following basic optimization information:

- Are indexes being used on the tables involved or was a tablespace scan selected?
- Which indexes specifically have been chosen?
- What is the order of the tables to process through?
- Are there any sorts involved?
- Why are there sorts?
- Which Join method has been chosen?
- Is there any materialization of views or nested table expressions, or common table expressions?
- Can just the Index file be accessed to fulfill the query or does DB2 also have to access the table's data file?
- More ...

19) Tools for Monitoring:

Just about every DB2 shop has a tool for DB2 monitoring that provides further detail on any given SQL statement or program. At times the monitoring tool is the only tool that can provide more specific guidance in finding a performance issue. Every DB2 SQL developer should become familiar with whatever DB2 monitoring tools their shop has installed. These tools will help answer some of the following questions. Some of the more common Z/OS DB2 monitoring tools are Omegamon, TMon, Mainview, Apptune, and DB2PM.

- Where is all the CPU being used (DB2, Stored Procedures, Application code, etc...)
- How many times is each SQL statement being executed
- How much time is being spent in Sort time
- Which SQL statement is causing the most slowness
- Are there any locking and concurrency issues
- I/O costs involved in getting the data needed
- Synchronous vs. Asynchronous processing costs
- Where is the CPU being used (DB2, Stored Procedures, Sort time, etc.)

Some of the more common DB2 UDB monitoring tools are IBM's Optim Query Tuner, Precise for DB2, Quest, DBI Software, Embarcadero Performance Analyst, ITGAIN, and others.

20) Employ Commit and Restart Strategies:

Every DB2 SQL batch developer should build a commit strategy into any programs that modify data. Failing to commit can cause locking, concurrency, and performance issues. If a program is modifying data, and some other program or process is trying to read or modify the same data, that program or process will get locked out. Along with commit strategies, there must also be restart strategies in abend situations so the program knows where to pick back up upon any restart.

An SQL Commit will apply all SQL modifications that have taken place (as of the last commit) and physically apply them to the data files. It will also release any locks that were being held. If another program is trying to process some of the same data that is being locked, DB2 puts that program into a wait queue until the lock frees up, or a certain amount of time has elapsed. The typical shop will only have DB2 hold requests in the queue for 30-45 seconds before it sends back a -911 SQL code to the requester. This is DB2's way of telling the program or process that it had tried to get some of the requested data, but found another process holding locks on the data over a designated wait time.

21) Index Design:

To create appropriate indexes, you really need to know the SQL that drives a particular application to best understand the access patterns. But many times the DBAs are called upon to create indexes well in advance of the creation of any SQL. Creating indexes to optimize SQL performance without any knowledge of the SQL is a challenging task. It makes it tough to create the proper indexes without an understanding of the SQL statements that will drive the application and how frequently each is to be executed. Part of tuning applications is creating and/or modifying indexes as application development is taking place, or once full-volume testing is in place.

There are some basic rules of thumb when creating indexes:

- Index by workload, not by object.
- Build indexes based on common query predicates.
- Definitely index the most heavily used queries.
- Create indexes for all primary and foreign key columns.
- Look to create indexes on columns frequently used in an ORDER BY, GROUP BY, or DISTINCT clause to avoid sorts.
- Consider overloading some indexes by adding columns to encourage index only access.
- Create indexes on columns that need to ensure uniqueness.
- Pay special attention to which index should be defined as the clustering index. See tuning tip #57.
- If the indexes take on more than one column, it is important to choose the order of the columns wisely. In general, the first column of the index should have a high cardinality.
- Columns frequently used together in a WHERE clause can benefit from a composite index to avoid maintaining multiple indexes.

continued…

Index Design cont...

Note: Examine the SQL that drives the application and look at all Insert, Update, and Delete activity. These statements will have implications on those indexes. If the columns of those indexes must be modified in any way, DB2 will incur additional overhead keeping the indexes up-to-date. For every Insert and Delete, not only will DB2 execute the action against the data, it has to also execute the action against every index, causing more overhead. So if an Insert statement executes on a table, and that table has five indexes defined, there will be six I/Os that take place to fulfill the insert request. One insert I/O to the base data file, and one each to each of the index files.

22) Avoid Discrepancies with Non Column Expressions.

When coding predicates that contain non column expressions, it is important to ensure that each expression's result is of the same definition as the column it is being compared to.

The optimizer determines the data type of the column on the left (for example, smallint). The optimizer then calculates the maximum size of the result of the expression on the right. If the maximum size of the result will fit into a smallint definition, then the predicate is Stage 1 and indexable. If the maximum could be too large to fit into a smallint definition or is a decimal and requires data conversion for the comparison, then the predicate is Stage 2 and non indexable.

The optimizer can cast down to compare a column to a smaller value, but it can't (yet) cast up to compare a column to a larger value. This is not always a problem in DB2 V8 since it has improved its comparing of numeric values with different data types, but it is a good habit to do for those cases that may not yet be covered.

For Example:

Where EDLEVEL = 123.45 * 12

   should be coded as

Where EDLEVEL = SMALLINT(Round(123.45*12,0))

This will execute the multiplication, round it to the whole number, and convert it to a smallint. Comparing the smallint column EDLEVEL to this value will be a Stage 1 indexable predicate.

23) Never put filtering logic within application code.

It is always best to have all the filtering logic that is needed written as predicates in a SQL statement. Do not leave some predicates out and have the database manger bring in extra rows and then eliminate / bypass some of the rows through program logic checks. (Some people call this Stage 3 processing).

Always start by putting all logic and filtering predicates in an SQL statement in order to get *exactly* the rows needed for the application, and *only* the rows needed. Use the power of the database manager's engine to perform the work of filtering. Deviate only when performance is an issue and all other efforts have not worked.

The same can be said of those processes that use a DB2 unload utility to dump a table of data into a flat file, and have a program process the data using the file. Use this only as a last resort when all other tuning efforts have failed.

24) Subquery predicates involving Min and Max can often be a Stage 2 predicate.

When coding a predicate that involves a subquery selecting a Min or Max value, make sure you know if the column in the predicate is defined as nullable or not. This can make a difference between the predicate being a Stage 1 versus a Stage 2 predicate. This is specific to the predicate operator being anything other than '='.

For example:

```
SELECT E.EMPNO, E.LASTNAME
FROM EMPLOYEE E
WHERE E.HIREDATE <=
      (SELECT MAX(T2.HIREDATE)
      FROM TABLE2 T2
      WHERE .....
      AND .....  )
```

If E.HIREDATE column is defined as 'Not Null', then this predicate becomes a Stage 2 predicate. The reason here is that the Min and Max functions can return a Null if no rows are found as part of its Where logic. The optimizer recognizes this and sets the predicate as Stage 2.

Developers should get in the habit of always coding a COALESCE or VALUE function on queries involving Min, Max, Sum, and Avg functions. DB2 will always return nulls as the answer if there are no rows found to calculate the function.

This is different when using the Count function. DB2 will return zeros if no rows are met in order to calculate a count.

continued...

Subquery predicates involving Min and Max cont...

To make this predicate a Stage 1 predicate, then recode it applying the VALUE or COALESCE function in the subquery.

For example:

```
SELECT E.EMPNO, E.LASTNAME
FROM EMPLOYEE E
WHERE E.HIREDATE <=
 (SELECT COALESCE(MAX(T2.HIREDATE), '9999-12-31')
   FROM TABLE2 T2
   WHERE .....
      AND .....  )
```

By applying the COALESCE function, DB2 will never return a Null out of the subquery. It will either return an actual Hiredate value, or return '9999-12-31'). The optimizer recognizes this and makes the predicate Stage 1 knowing that there will always be some value returned out of the subquery, no matter if rows are found based on the 'Where' criteria or not.

25) Always code 'For Fetch Only' or 'For Read Only' with cursor processing when a query is only selecting data.

There is something in the DB2 retrieval process called Block Fetching. Block Fetching can significantly decrease the number of messages sent across the network, and is used only with cursors that will not update or delete data. With Block Fetching, DB2 groups the rows that are retrieved by an SQL query into as large a block of rows as will fit in a message buffer. DB2 then transmits the block over the network, without requiring a separate message for each row.

To have DB2 take advantage of the block fetch process, DB2 must determine that a cursor is not used for updating or deleting. The easiest way to indicate that the cursor does not modify data is to add the FOR FETCH ONLY or FOR READ ONLY clause to the query. Without this statement, DB2 defines the cursor as an Ambiguous Cursor, and turns off Block Fetching.

Specifying 'For Read Only' can also improve the performance of FETCH operations because DB2 can avoid exclusive locks and guarantee that selected data will not be modified, preventing some types of deadlocks.

26) Stay away from Selecting a row from a table to help decide whether the logic in the code should then execute an Update or an Insert.

Selecting a row requires an extra call to DB2. If the code updates more than it inserts during a run, then it should skip any Select and go right into an Update. If the Update statement receives a +100 'Not Found' error, then execute the Insert.

If the code executes more inserts than updates, then skip any Select and go right into an Insert. If the Insert statement receives a -803 'Duplicate Insert' error, then execute the Update.

Be aware that a -803 errors has significant overhead involved, and too many of them can affect performance. Caution should be taken to understand how many records will be inserted versus updated.

Be aware that DB2 V9 introduces a SQL Merge statement that will also be more efficient. The Merge can specify what to do on a matched condition (an UPDATE) or a non-matched condition (an INSERT).

27) Stay away from Selecting a row from a table in order to get values for an update.

Developers do not have to retrieve data first, and manipulate it, before executing the Update. Doing so requires an extra call to DB2.

For example, suppose an employee is to be given a 10% raise, instead of selecting the employee's Salary, adding 10% to the value, and then using the new value in an update statement, the update statement should look like:

UPDATE EMPLOYEE
SET SALARY = SALARY * 1.1
WHERE EMPNO = ?

28) Make use of Dynamic SQL statement caching.

For languages like Java, Crystal Reporting, Visual Basic and many others that execute dynamic SQL statements, DB2 determines the access path (optimization) at run time when the statement is prepared. This can make the performance worse than that of static SQL statements. However, if an application executes the same SQL statement often, it can use the dynamic statement cache to decrease the number of times that those dynamic statements are prepared.

When shops have Dynamic SQL Caching set to 'On', then that statement's prepared optimization is stored in the system's cache for any future executions of the same statement, either by the same process or another process executing the statement with a different value. But any subsequent SQL statement being executed must match the cached SQL statement exactly, except for the values in the host variables.

So for languages that execute Dynamic SQL statements, it's important to Prepare the SQL statement with input host variables before the host variables actually have values placed in them. If values are moved into the host variables, and then the statement is prepared, the optimization is done using the actual values. In that case, every subsequent time the statement is executed using a different value, there will be another prepare because the statement is different than any previous one. It can also fill up the cache, causing performance issues for others sharing the cache.

29) Avoid 'Select *'

Using 'Select *' isn't quite so bad for one time queries, but is definitely not wanted when part of application development code. Programmers code SQL to select data into host variables fields within their code. When they code 'Select *' they have to code a host variable for each column in the table.

What if the table drops a column, or the tables get a new column added? If this happens, then the source code would need to be changed. To avoid this possibility, do not use 'Select *' in the first place.

Developers do not typically need every column from a table being queried. By having extra columns that are not really used can cause optimization and efficiency issues. Refer to tuning tip #3.

30) Watch out for nullable columns, or times when nulls can be returned from the database manager.

Most languages handle nulls pretty well, although Cobol is very problematic. If the SQL or the Cobol code is not set up to handle nulls correctly, the Cobol program will get a -305 SQLCODE which typically takes it to an error routine.

But no matter the development language, if the logic is not set up to expect the possibility of nulls, then logic errors may occur. Following are some areas where nulls can occur.

- Columns can be defined as nullable in the table definition
- Case statements without an 'Else'
- Left, Right, Full outer joins
- Select Min, Max, Avg, Sum
- Mathematics involving a nullable column

Cobol developers should always try to eliminate any nulls from coming into the program by using the VALUE or COALESCE scalar functions whenever possible. This keeps the Cobol developers from having to code and check null indicators after every Select or Fetch.

This is extremely important for developers to know. There is way too many incident reports and abends in daily production specifically due to the developers not knowing that nulls could occur, and not coding for them.

31) Minimize the number of times Open and Close cursors are executed.

Opening and closing a cursor creates much more overhead than a Select Statement. If most of time a Select statement returns only 1 row of data, then there is no need to execute cursor processing.

Logic should be set up in these scenarios to first execute a Select statement and see if 1 or more rows are returned. If more than 1 row is returned to a select Statement, an -811 SQLCODE is also returned.

For these cases where a -811 is retuned, capture this specific return code and then execute cursor processing. By coding program logic this way, cursor processing is only being executed for those times with multiple rows. All other times, a simple Select statement get executed.

32) Avoid 'Not' logic in SQL.

Not logic is very inefficient in the SQL language. Take for example the following:

SELECT EMPNO, LASTNAME
FROM EMPLOYEE
WHERE NOT HIREDATE < '2000-01-01'

Applying the Not logic against a column reduces the SQL predicate to Non Indexable and Stage 2. Keep the SQL predicates coded in a positive manner.

SELECT EMPNO, LASTNAME
FROM EMPLOYEE
WHERE HIREDATE >= '2000-01-01'

33) Use correlation Ids for better readability.

There is nothing more frustrating than working on someone's SQL statement that is not written neatly or contains no correlation IDs. This is not much of a problem when the query contains only a couple of tables, but can get very confusing with multiple tables and more involved SQL statements.

Also, use correlation IDs that make sense for the table they refer to. Do not use the typical A, B, C, D, etc...

For Example, E for the Employee table, D for the Department table:

```
SELECT E.EMPNO, E.LASTNAME
FROM EMPLOYEE E
 WHERE EXISTS
      (SELECT 1
       FROM DEPARTMENT D
       WHERE D.MGRNO = E.EMPNO
       AND D.DEPTNO LIKE 'D%')
```

There are websites that will take SQL code and format it nice and neat. Go to Google and type in 'SQL Formatter' and some sites will come up where you can paste a SQL statement and have it come back aligned, indented, and readable.

Correlation Ids should especially be coded in all correlated subqueries in the join predicate. There are times in subqueries that logic can be different depending on these correlations IDs being present or not in the join statement within the subquery.

34) Keep Table and Index files healthy and organized.

Maintaining the table and index files is one of the many tasks assigned to DBAs. Both data and indexes are contained in their own files. As more and more activity is executed against these files, they become unorganized, fragmented and extended.

There are many utilities that come with DB2 to assists in maintaining the physical files. Using these utilities wisely can have a huge effect on performance. The most common utility for cleaning up data and index files is the 'Reorg'. The REORG utility can be used to reorganize DB2 table spaces and indexes, thereby improving the efficiency of access to those objects. Reorganization is required periodically to ensure that the data is situated in an optimal fashion for subsequent access.

This is one of the many tasks typically assigned to DBAs, and most of the time they do a very good job of monitoring and executing the 'Reorg' utility to keep files healthy. But it is still one more item to look into when performance is an issue.

Indexes are also files, and need to be maintained. A 'Reorg' on an index file keeps them efficiently clustered which can affect access performance and index choices from the optimizer.

35) In Cobol, take advantage of 'Update where Current of Cursor' and 'Delete Where Current of Cursor'.

The Cobol language has some options other languages do not. One of the options is to execute an Update or Delete statement during cursor processing. There are two ways to execute these. One way is to branch off and execute the Update or Delete specific to the key fields just fetched in the cursor. This is often called a 'Positioned' update.

The other way is to take advantage of the cursor positioning and execute the Update or Delete, which is much more efficient.

Many times cursor processing in Cobol is by default 'Read Only' cursors where the developer may not be able to take advantage of 'Update Where Current of Cursor'. The typical 'Read Only' cursor is when the cursor definition has an 'Order By' statement. But with the advantage of the Dynamic Scrollable cursors, 'Delete Where Current of Cursor' can still be executed when coded with an 'Order By statement. See tuning tip #43.

There are different locking issues involved here when a cursor is specified with 'For Update Of', affecting concurrency with the data involved. But if this is not an issue, declaring your cursor to take advantage of 'Update where Current of Cursor' or 'Delete Where Current of Cursor' will process faster.

36) When using cursors, use ROWSET positioning and fetching using multi row fetch, multi row update, and multi row insert.

DB2 V8 introduced support for the manipulation of multiple rows on fetches, updates, and insert processing. Prior versions of DB2 would only allow for a program to process one row at a time during cursor processing. Now having the ability to fetch, update, or insert more than 1 row at a time reduces network traffic and other related costs associated with each call to DB2.

When fetching data from a cursor, developers can code to fetch, say, 100 rows at a time with one fetch statement by fetching the data into an array for each host variables. 100 rows at a time seems to be the threshold. More than 100 has diminishing returns as far as efficiency. The recommendation is to start with 100 row fetches, inserts, or updates, and then test other numbers. It has been proven many times that this process reduces runtime an average of 35%. Consult the IBM DB2 manuals for further detail and coding examples.

For local applications, using these multiple-row statements results in fewer accesses of the database. For distributed applications, using these multiple-row statements results in fewer network operations and a significant improvement in performance.

See tuning tips #46, #47, and #48 for coding examples.

37) Know Your Locking Isolation Levels:

DB2 offers four isolation locking levels: Repeatable read (RR), Read Stability (RS), Cursor Stability (CS) and Uncommitted Read (UR). Each of these isolation levels allows the user and application to control the number and duration of read (Share) locks held within a unit of work. By setting the appropriate isolation level based on a particular application's requirement, lock resources can be minimized and the user/program concurrency can be increased. Take the following example:

```
SELECT LAST_NAME, EMPLOYEE_NUMBER
FROM EMPLOYEE
WHERE LAST_NAME LIKE `S%'
WITH RR, RS, CS, UR
```

With RR: Repeatable Read means that the same query can be executed multiple times within the same unit-of-work and the results of the query will be identical every time (repeatable). A Share lock will be set and stay on each row or page until the query or logical unit of work has completed. All accessed rows or pages are locked even if they do not satisfy the predicate. For table scans, this would encompass each row/page within the table.

For other queries not processing table scans, this would encompass any rows or pages that meet the predicate criteria of the SQL statement. In the example, this would be all rows or pages containing last names that begin with 'S'.

continued...

Know Your Locking Levels cont...

All share locks with RR are held until a commit takes place. These share locks would effectively prevent updates, insert, or deletes (X locks) from occurring on any of the rows/pages from any other process until a commit is executed.

Note on 'RR': Most query tools on the market have their default isolation level set to 'RR', which is not good. This causes many problems in environments where users, analysts, developers, and others query the data often during the day. Many times users leave their workstations while a query is running in the background which is applying and holding locks on the data being retrieved. This is a common reason for many -911 Sqlcode errors.

With RS: Read Stability is very much like the 'RR' except that it will allow inserts from other users. It can at times lock more rows/pages because locks are taken and held on data, even when it goes to Stage 2 processing to further check predicates. If there is a Stage 2 predicate and the data does not fit the predicate criteria, the 'RS' lock is still placed and held.

continued...

Know Your Locking Levels cont...

With CS: Cursor Stability sets a Share lock on each row or page processed, and the moment the cursor moves on to another row or page, it releases the lock. So at any one time there is only one lock being held either on a row or page of data. This obviously allows good concurrency and some data integrity. Almost all batch Cobol programs in IT shops today are bound with the locking parameter of 'CS'. This is because as these programs execute cursor processing, they have no need to reread any data processed. The share locks get freed up as it moves through the cursor and has data integrity as it processes each current row or page. This bind parameter along with another bind parameter 'Currentdata(No)' provides an opportunity for avoiding locks altogether. With these 2 bind parameter together, DB2 can test to see if a row or page has committed data on it, and if it has, DB2 will not have to obtain any lock .

With UR: Uncommitted Read means that no Share locks are placed on any rows or pages processed by this query, and it does not matter if other processes have any locks on any of the data being retrieved. This can improve efficiency because it reduces overall processing time. But the one issue in using UR is that if some other process has applied updates to data being retrieved, UR will return their updated data from the buffer before the other process has executed a commit. If for some reason the other process does a Rollback of its updates, then this UR process has updated data that was never committed.

continued...

Know Your Locking Levels cont...

Even with the issue of possibly picking up non-committed data, there are definitely times when UR can be used:

1) Data warehouse queries. Typically no updates take place in these environments.

2) OLAP/OLTP processing. If most update processing is done in nightly batch, then having all OLAP/OLTP process with UR provides better performance and response time automatically due to no locking taking place.

3) Works well querying tables that rarely change, like codes and reference tables.

4) Query Tools when executing dynamic queries throughout the day, UR will not interfere with production processing by placing Share locks on data.

38) Know Your Null Processing.

Developers need to know and understand Null processing, especially Cobol programmers. The Cobol language does not handle a null returned from DB2 as nicely as other languages. If a Cobol program receives a null from DB2 and the program is not set up to handle the null by using a null indicator, or having coded using VALUE or COALESCE, then DB2 returns a -305 error.

Example 1:

```
SELECT EMPNO,
SALARY + BONUS + COMM AS TOTAL_ PAY
FROM EMPLOYEE
```

If any of the columns Salary, Bonus or Comm is null then the answer for Total_Pay come back as null. Should be coded as:

```
SELECT EMPNO,
        COALESCE (SALARY,0)  +
        COALESCE (BONUS, 0)  +
        COALESCE (COMM,  0)  AS TOTAL_ PAY
FROM EMPLOYEE
```

continued…

Know Your Null Processing cont...

Example 2:

```
SELECT DEPTNO, AVG(SALARY)
FROM EMPLOYEE
WHERE DEPTNO = 'XYZ'
```

If no rows are found, then the answer comes back as null.
Should be coded as follows:

```
SELECT DEPTNO,
COALESCE(AVG(SALARY),0)
FROM EMPLOYEE
WHERE DEPTNO = 'XYZ'
```

Example 3:

```
SELECT EMPNO, SALARY, BONUS, COMM
FROM EMPLOYEE
WHERE BONUS <> COMM
```

If one of the columns has a value and the other is null, that does not make them unequal and part of the result set.

continued...

Know Your Null Processing cont...

If one of them has a value, and the other may not, and the developer wants them to be part of the result set due to not being equal, the query could be coded as follow. Note however that this predicate now becomes a Stage 2 predicate.

```
SELECT EMPNO, SALARY, BONUS, COMM
FROM EMPLOYEE
WHERE  COALESCE(BONUS,1) <>
         COALESCE(COMM,0)
```

Or as of Version 8. You could code:

```
SELECT EMPNO, SALARY, BONUS, COMM
FROM EMPLOYEE
WHERE BONUS IS DISTINCT FROM COMM
```

Cobol programmers need to know when nulls can be returned as part of the answer set, and try to eliminate them by coding the COALESCE or VALUE scalar functions. The -305 SQL error is a very common problem in Cobol production systems.

39) Always program with performance in mind.

Programmers should always have two goals in mind when developing programs and applications for user groups.

- To get the correct results for requested data
- To get the results back as quickly as possible

So many times programmers today lose sight of the second goal. They either do not know what to do to get programs to run faster, blame other pieces of their environment (database, network, TCP/IP, etc.), or think that the time spent processing the data was pretty good based on the amount of data. They need to always be sure their program is running as efficiently as possible. If they are not sure, then they should consult colleagues. The many tuning tips in this book will certainly give them a starting point. The one thing programmers should always know is how much data was processed base on the runtime. Did the program process 100,000 rows of data or 10 million rows of data? How many updates, inserts, deletes, selects, open cursors, commits, etc. should be noted as part of each output.

If a program has a performance issue, the first question is typically 'How much data is being processed'? Every program should note somewhere the amount of data that was processed, and log or display this somewhere to fall back on.

40) Let SQL do the work.

This is what is called 'Relational Programming' versus 'Procedural Programming'. Too many times developers do the following:

- Break up their joins or cursors. Joining tables *outside* of DB2 is typically not smart or efficient SQL
- Execute separate 'Exists' logic
- Execute separate 'Selects' for code descriptions
- Execute their own rounding logic
- Execute their own truncating logic
- Execute their own concatenation logic
- Execute their own mathematics, string functions, etc. in their code

Developers should take advantage of DB2 SQL Scalar functions in order to get data exactly as needed for their output. Using Scalar functions as part of the 'Select' clause in SQL does not cause jobs to run long, whereas using them on columns in predicates can be a big performance issue. Developers should always code their queries in a Query Tool first, get the data back exactly as needed, then move the query to their program. Most programs should simply be SQL fetches and code moves with no other routines being executed in between.

Always try to get what is needed into one SQL statement, and then break it up if performance is an issue, even if it requires a 5 or 10 table join. Do not execute singleton selects in order to check existence or to get code descriptions. Build this logic into the SQL statement.

41) Lock Table:

Many time developers have programs that execute multiple SQL Update, Insert and/or Delete statements. Often when these statements execute, there is a DB2 lock that takes place. Locks are a big part of overall performance and runtime, so the more locks that take place the longer processes execute. Typically DBAs have thresholds in place to keep developers from processing too many locks. They set a threshold option to escalate the locking to a tablespace lock and letting the program continue, or set a threshold to cause the program to abend.

By coding a 'Lock Table' statement before processing, one exclusive lock is taken at the table level. Because this is a higher level lock than a row or page, all individual locks on update, insert, or deletes are alleviated. This will make the program execute much faster, but the entire table is locked up by the program for the duration of it runtime.

For example the Lock Table may help a program execute in 10 minutes instead of 30-40 due to one tablespace lock versus many individual row or page locks. But during those 10 minutes everyone else is locked out in processing against that table, unless they use 'With UR'.

continued…

Lock Table cont...

For example:

LOCK TABLE EMPLOYEE IN EXCLUSIVE MODE

LOCK TABLE EMPLOYEE PART 10 IN EXCLUSIVE
 MODE

Using the Lock Table statement is especially efficient when a program is going to set locks that affect 25% or more of the data in a table.

42) OLTP Front End Processing.

When executing SQL statements out of front end OLTP programs that may return multiple rows, consider trying the 'Optimize for n Rows' statement to influence the optimizer to choose the best access path based on the number. This should be tried especially when the number of rows needed is significantly less than the total number of rows that may be returned. For example:

SELECT EMPNO, LASTNAME, DEPTNO, SALARY
FROM EMPLOYEE
WHERE DEPTNO > ?
OPTIMIZE FOR 14 ROWS

If you know for sure that your screen will only process 100 rows no matter how many get returned, then the SQL statement should specify 'Fetch First 100 Rows Only'. See tuning tip #65. For example:

SELECT EMPNO, LASTNAME, DEPTNO, SALARY
FROM EMPLOYEE
WHERE DEPTNO > ?
FETCH FIRST 100 ROWS ONLY

This statement will often disable 'List Prefetch' in its optimization which causes the optimizer to bypass a sorting of index RIDs before accessing data.

continued...

OLTP Front End Processing cont...

List Prefetch is usually good because the RID sort helps minimize the number of 'Getpage' request in retrieving the data. But most OLTP processes do not process much data, so the added sort can be extra runtime that does not add much help to its process. It may be more efficient for OLTP processes to bypass this RID sort.

Applying the 'Optimize for n Rows' in no way affects the logic of the SQL statement.

43) Consider using Dynamic Scrollable Cursors:

Scrollable cursors were introduced in V7. Now DB2 V8 introduced Dynamic Scrollable Cursors which increases performance.

Dynamic scrollable cursors enable direct access to the data in the base table instead of having to use a declared temporary table (materialization). Each FETCH returns the most current data and is sensitive to all INSERTs, UPDATEs, and DELETEs (meaning no more delete holes and missing updates as seen from scrollable cursors). With regular scrollable cursors, temporary table are created and the data selection from the cursor is materialized into the table. This is overhead. If we can process the data without the overhead of DB2 creating a temporary file, loading the file, then processing it, it is an automatic performance boost. For Example:

DECLARE CURSOR1 SENSITIVE **DYNAMIC** SCROLL
CURSOR FOR
    SELECT C1, C2
    FROM T1;

Using a dynamic scrollable cursor, you can fetch newly inserted rows but you cannot fetch deleted rows. In contrast, with a static scrollable cursor, you cannot fetch newly inserted rows, and rows that have been deleted are indicated as holes in the result table of the cursor. Because the associated FETCH statement using the dynamic scrollable cursor executes on the base table, the cursor needs no temporary result table.

continued…

Dynamic Scrollable Cursors cont...

When you define a cursor as SENSITIVE DYNAMIC, you cannot specify the INSENSITIVE keyword in a FETCH statement for that cursor.

There are definitely some performance gains when using dynamic scrollable cursors:

1) Sometimes, there will be no materialization of data into a work file. No materialization will take place if no 'Order By' is coded as part of the SQL statement, or the optimizer can satisfy a specified 'Order By' by using an associated index.

2) If you specify an ORDER BY clause for a SENSITIVE DYNAMIC cursor, DB2 might choose an index access path if the ORDER BY is fully satisfied by an existing index. However, a dynamic scrollable cursor that is declared with an ORDER BY cannot 'Update where Current of Cursor', but can 'Delete Where Current of Cursor'.

Processing a non scrollable cursor with an 'Order By' automatically makes a cursor 'Read Only' and stops the processing from being allowed to update or delete 'Where Current of Cursor' statements. But by defining a cursor as a 'Sensitive Dynamic Scroll' it allows the process to execute 'Delete Where Current of Cursor' statements. Anytime a process can update or delete 'Where Current of Cursor' as opposed to executing individual update or delete statements always helps processes to execute faster.

44. Take advantage of Materialized Query Tables to improve response time:

A materialized query table, or MQT, is basically a view whose data is materialized and saved into a table. So, you can turn a view into a table using MQTs, providing potential benefit for many complex queries (especially those performing summaries and analytics). Of course, there are management issues involved, but you can use MQTs to create denormalized or aggregated structures to improve query performance, and leave the base tables fully normalized.

Both views and MQTs are defined on the basis of a query. The query on which a view is based is run whenever the view is referenced; however, an MQT actually stores the query results as data, and you can work with the data that is in the MQT instead of the data that is in the underlying tables.

Materialized query tables can significantly improve the performance of queries, especially complex queries. If the optimizer determines that a query or part of a query could be resolved using an MQT, the query may get rewritten by the optimizer to take advantage of the MQT. This is called 'Automatic Query Rewrite'.

continued...

Materialized Query Tables cont..

Why MQTs? They are specifically for improving performance. When SQL queries are coded against denormalized or aggregated data structures (like many MQTs), I/O is saved relating directly to performance gains.

Overview

- MQTs are tables that typically contain derived information
- MQTs may store pre-calculated or summarized data
- MQTs may be derived from expensive SQL such as joins or complex aggregation
- With automatic query rewrite (AQR), DB2 considers an MQT in place of underlying tables coded in SQL queries
- Great for Dynamic SQL Queries
- MQTs are physical and can be processed directly
- Pre-computed data gets externalized into a MQT
- Indexes can be created on MQTs

continued…

Materialized Query Tables cont...

Example:

```
CREATE TABLE DEPT_SUM_MQT_TABLE AS
(SELECT DEPTNO, AVG(SALARY) AS AVG_SAL,
 AVG(BONUS) AS AVG_BONUS
 AVG(COMM)  AS AVG_COMM,
 SUM(SALARY AS SUM_SAL,
 SUM(BONUS) AS SUM_BONUS
 SUM(COMM)  AS SUM_COMM
 FROM EMPLOYEE
 GROUP BY DEPTNO)

 DATA INITIALLY DEFERRED REFRESH DEFERRED
 MAINTAINED BY SYSTEM ENABLE QUERY
 OPTIMIZATION;
```

Notes: There are different values that can be specified for the 'Deferred' and 'Maintained' parts of the Create statement. The 'Maintained by System' means that the system will keep this table in check with the underlying table(s) as any insert, update, or deletes takes place that may affect the data in the MQT. Check the IBM manuals for full descriptions.

continued...

Materialized Query Tables cont...

With the 'Enable Query Optimization' specified, if a query gets coded as follows:

```
SELECT SUMM(BONUS)
FROM EMPLOYEE
 WHERE DEPTNO = 'A00'
```

the optimizer will actually rewrite it to be:

```
SELECT AVG_BONUS
FROM DEPT_SUM_MQT_TABLE
WHERE DEPTNO = 'A00'
```

DB2 choosing to rewrite and select the data off the MQT summary table will be much more efficient than gathering all the 'A00' rows off the base table, summarizing the Bonus column, and then returning the result. By processing against the MQT, there will be one row in that table for department 'A00' that already contains the sum for the Bonus column, reducing the amount of I/O.

45. Insert with Select.

You can now select what was just inserted with the same statement saving multiple calls to DB2. This again is what is called 'Relational' programming instead of 'Procedural' programming. In procedural programming a developer would execute the insert statement, and then send another select statement back to DB2 to view the results of the insert. Relational programming is thinking of how can I get what is needed while making the minimal number of SQL calls to DB2. This Insert with Select is a great technique for retrieving values from columns that get created or modified by DB2 during an insert process, and are needed for further processing in a program.

For example, they can retrieve the following values:

- Identity columns or sequence values that get automatically
  assigned by DB2
- User-defined defaults and expressions that are not known
  to the developer
- Columns modified by triggers that can vary from insert
  to insert depending on values
- ROWIDs, CURRENT TIMESTAMP that are assigned
  automatically

continued…

Insert with Select cont...

Example:

```
SELECT C1, C2, C5, C6, C8, C11, C12
FROM FINAL TABLE
 (INSERT (C2, C3, C4, C5, C6, C8, C10)
  VALUES ('ABC', 123.12, 'A', 'DEF',
              50000.00, 'GHI', '2008-01-01')
 )
```

The words 'Final Table' are SQL DB2 reserved words that need to be coded for this statement to work. This example shows selecting other columns that were not part of the insert statement. These could be columns that get derived through a Trigger, are defaults values, or automatically assigned sequence numbers.

This is most helpful when inserting into Parent/Child tables. The parent get inserted first, and if DB2 automatically assign a sequence number or identity value as part of the primary key, then this value needs to used in all the Child inserts also. Being able to retrieve this value right away as part of the insert saves extra calls back to DB2 in order to get the sequence or identity value.

46. Take Advantage of Multi Row Fetch.

You can now fetch multiple rows from DB2 with one fetch statement using arrays. For years in DB2 SQL, arrays could not be used in an SQL statement. That has changed as of V8. Now, using arrays defined in Cobol working storage for each column being selected, one FETCH statement sent to DB2 can return many rows at one time. The program then processes those rows using its own array logic. The DECLARE CURSOR SQL statement has a new keyword added just for this purpose.

WITH ROWSET POSITIONING tells DB2 at cursor open that this cursor allows multi-row processing. Even if you define the cursor for multi-row processing, you still have the option to fetch one row at a time. It would simply be a 1-row rowset. Multi row fetching will improve throughput by having fewer database access calls and lowering network operations and has been shown to reduce CPU consumption. Most testing has shown an average of 35% increase in performance. Currently performance gains begin with 10 rows per fetch, and peak at 100 rows per fetch. Anything over 100 has typically shown diminishing returns. Developers should begin with 100.

continued…

Multi Row Fetch cont..

For Example: Set up arrays for each column and null indicator that is to be selected and execute the fetch into the arrays. Each column in the Select must have its own array and any associated null indicator array. DB2 will give you all the information you need, like row counts and SQLCODEs via the new V8 SQL statement **GET DIAGNOSTICS** to aid in deciphering what was placed in the array by DB2. See the IBM manuals for further information. This should be an SQL Standard in any shop's Standards and Guidelines for SQL programming. I prefer developers to use the COALECSE or VALUE scalar function in place of coding null indicators.

```
01  HV-NUM-ROWS          PIC S9(4) COMP.
01  HOST-VARIABLES.
  05  HV-EMPNO-ARRAY  PIC X(6)
                          OCCURS 100 TIMES.
  05  HV-LASTNAME-ARRAY OCCURS 100 TIMES.
    49  HV-LASTNAME-LENGTH  PIC S9(4) COMP.
    49  HV-LASTNAME-TEXT   PIC X(25).
  05  HV-SALARY-ARRAY   PIC S9(7)V9(2)
                          OCCURS 100 TIMES.
  05  HV-BONUS-ARRAY    PIC S9(7)V9(2)
                          OCCURS 100 TIMES.
  05  HV-BONUS-NI-ARRAY PIC S9(4) COMP
                          OCCURS 100 TIMES.
```

continued…

Multi Row Fetch cont..

DECLARE EMP_CSR CURSOR **WITH ROWSET POSITIONING**
   FOR SELECT EMPNO, LASTNAME,
         SALARY, BONUS
   FROM EMPLOYEE
   WHERE EMPNO > '000050'

 OPEN EMP_CSR ;

MOVE +100 TO HV-NUM-ROWS

FETCH NEXT ROWSET FROM EMP_CSR
                 FOR :HV-NUM-ROWS ROWS
INTO :HV-EMPNO-ARRAY,
     :HV-LASTNAME-ARRAY,
     :HV-SALARY-ARRAY,
     :HV-BONUS-ARRAY :HV-BONUS-NI-ARRAY

The program would then use its own logic to loop through the arrays and process the data. The DB2 SQLCA communication area contains a field called SQLERRD (3) that will contain how many rows were actually returned on each fetch.

47. Take Advantage of Multi Row Insert.

With V8 you can send many insert statements stacked up in host variable arrays to DB2 with one insert statement. With DB2 for z/OS we have had two ways using SQL to get rows into a table. You could insert one row at a time using the INSERT with a VALUES clause or insert multiple rows via an INSERT that included a SELECT clause from another table. Until now we have had no way to insert multiple rows with a single statement.

DB2 V8 will use arrays, similar to FETCH processing, to insert more than one row into a DB2 table with a single INSERT SQL statement. Multi-row INSERT is absolutely supported for distributed applications and should be considered to improve the overall performance of INSERT processing. Most testing has shown on average of 20% increase in performance.

For Example: Set up arrays for each column and null indicator, load up the array, then send one insert statement to DB2. Keep in mind that if there are any errors on any of the entries, a DB2 SQL 'Get Diagnostics' command will be needed in order to see which entries were in error. See the IBM manuals for further information.

continued…

Multi Row Insert cont...

For Example:

```
01  HV-NUM-ROWS              PIC S9(4) COMP.
01  HOST-VARIABLES.
   05  HV-EMPNO-ARRAY PIC X(6)
                            OCCURS 100 TIMES.
    05  HV-LASTNAME-ARRAY OCCURS 100 TIMES.
     49  HV-LASTNAME-LENGTH  PIC S9(4) COMP.
     49  HV-LASTNAME-TEXT    PIC X(25).
  05  HV-SALARY-ARRAY      PIC S9(7)V9(2)
                            OCCURS 100 TIMES.
  05  HV-BONUS-ARRAY    PIC S9(7)V9(2)
                            OCCURS 100 TIMES.
  05 HV-BONUS-NI-ARRAY PIC S9(4) COMP
                            OCCURS 100 TIMES.
```

The program loads up the arrays with data to be inserted, then executes the following SQL statement.

```
MOVE +100 TO HV-NUM-ROWS.
  INSERT INTO EMPLOYEE
  (EMPNO, LASTNAME, FIRSTNME,
  MIDINIT, SALARY, BONUS)
VALUES (:HV-EMPNO-ARRAY,
     :HV-LASTNAME-ARRAY,
     :HV-SALARY-ARRAY,
     :HV-BONUS-ARRAY:HV-BONUS-NI-ARRAY)
 FOR :HV-NUM-ROWS
 ATOMIC
```

continued ...

Multi Row Insert cont...

The new keyword, ATOMIC, tells DB2 what to do if an error should occur during an INSERT. When coding a multiple row INSERT statement, you can specify ATOMIC (the default), or NOT ATOMIC CONTINUE ON SQLEXCEPTION. ATOMIC turns on the all or nothing switch. This means that if any INSERT fails as part of the array, all INSERTs for this SQL statement (even those that completed successfully) will be rolled back. If NOT ATOMIC CONTINUE ON SQLEXCEPTION is specified, any successfully inserted row prior to the row in error remains, and no rollback is attempted. The INSERT will also continue in attempting to insert the remaining rows in the array. Only the individual rows with errors are not inserted. The SQL GET DIAGNOSTICS statement is used to determine which rows were not successfully inserted.

For dynamic SQL, developers must specify 'For Multiple Rows' during the Prepare, and 'For N Rows' and 'Using' for the list of variables in the Execute. See the IBM manuals for further information.

48. Take Advantage of Multi Row Update.

You can now update many rows stacked up in host variable arrays to DB2 with one update statement. Multi-row updating will improve throughput by having fewer database access calls and lowering network operations. It has been shown to reduce CPU consumption. The performance gain here is the efficiency of the Multi-Row Fetches, and possibly the updating of the whole rowset with one update statement.

But watch out for which update gets executed.

Update where current of ….

1) 'Update Where Current of Cursor' will update every row in the array
2) 'Update Where Current of Cursor for Row 12 of Rowset' will update the 12th row in the array.

For Example: This will fetch 100 rows at a time, and update all 100 at a time by giving each a 10% raise in their salary.

```
DECLARE EMP_CSR  CURSOR WITH HOLD WITH
                          ROWSET POSITIONING FOR
     SELECT EMPNO, SALARY, BONUS
     FROM  EMPLOYEE
     WHERE EMPNO > '000040'
     FOR UPDATE OF SALARY;
```

continued …

Multi Row Update cont...

```
OPEN EMP_CSR ;

MOVE +100 TO HV-NUM-ROWS
FETCH NEXT ROWSET FROM EMP_CSR FOR
                        :HV-NUM-ROWS ROWS
INTO :HV-EMPNO-ARRAY,
  :HV-SALARY_ARRAY,
  :HV-BONUS-ARRAY :HV-BONUS-NI-ARRAY ;

UPDATE EMPLOYEE
  SET SALARY = SALARY * 1.1
  WHERE CURRENT OF EMP_CSR;

CLOSE CURSOR2;
```

Note: This is great as long as every row gets updated the same way. But what if each row fetched gets their salary updated differently? In that case each row in the rowset would have to get updated individually. For example, fetching a rowset of 100 into host variable arrays, and each having their salary adjusted by different formulas would have to get updated individually.

continued ...

Multi Row Update cont...

For example: To update each row differently:

```
MOVE SQLERRD(3) TO WS-FETCHED-CNT

PERFORM VARYING SUB1 FROM 1 BY 1 UNTIL
   SUB1 >  WS-FETCHED-CNT
     MOVE HV-SALARY-ARRAY (SUB1) TO HV-SALARY
     UPDATE EMPLOYEE
     SET SALARY = :HV-SALARY
   WHERE CURRENT OF EMP_CSR  FOR ROW :SUB1
     OF ROWSET
END-PERFORM
```

49. Take Advantage of Multi Row Delete.

You can now delete many rows stacked up in host variable arrays to DB2 with one delete statement. Multi row deleting will improve throughput by having fewer database access calls and lowering network operations, and has shown to reduce CPU consumption. It works just like the Multi-Row Update. The performance gain here is the efficiency of the Multi-Row Fetches, and possibly the deleting of the whole rowset with one delete statement.

But watch out for which delete statement gets executed.

1) 'DELETE WHERE CURRENT OF EMP_CSR' will
    delete every row in the rowset array
2) 'DELETE WHERE CURRENT OF EMP_CSR FOR
    ROW 12 OF ROWSET' will delete the 12th row in the
    rowset array.

50. Use Scalar Fullselects within the Select clause:

Many times the output needed from SQL development requires a combination of detail and aggregate data together. There are typically a number of ways to code this with SQL, but with the Scalar Fullselect now part of DB2 V8, there is now another option that is very efficient as long as indexes are being used. Suppose a report is needed to get employee salaries along with the average salary of the department that they work in. This requires detail data along with average salary by department aggregated together. For example, using the new Scalar Fullselect:

```
SELECT E1.EMPNO, E1.LASTNAME,
    E1.WORKDEPT, E1.SALARY,
    (SELECT AVG(E2.SALARY)
     FROM EMPLOYEE E2
     WHERE E2.WORKDEPT = E1.WORKDEPT)
                        AS DEPT_AVG_SAL
FROM EMPLOYEE E1
ORDER BY E1.WORKDEPT, E1.SALARY
```

Prior to V8, this logic had to be coded using an SQL nested table expression, requiring materialization of the 'X' table before the join process. With V8, the nested table expression can now be rewritten as a common table expression using the 'With' expression for table 'X'. Following are examples of how this query had to be coded before, and how it can be coded with common table expression. Typically the new Scalar Fullselect runs much faster.

continued …

Scalar Fullselects cont...

Old Nested Table Expression:

```
SELECT E.EMPNO,    E.LASTNAME,
    E.WORKDEPT,    E.SALARY,    X.DEPT_AVG_SAL
FROM EMPLOYEE E,
    (SELECT WORKDEPT, AVG(E2.SALARY) AS
                                DEPT_AVG_SAL
    FROM EMPLOYEE E2
    GROUP BY WORKDEPT) AS X
WHERE E.WORKDEPT = X.WORKDEPT
ORDER BY E.WORKDEPT, E.SALARY
```

Newer Common Table Expression:

```
With X as
(SELECT WORKDEPT, AVG(E2.SALARY) AS
                                DEPT_AVG_SAL
    FROM EMPLOYEE E2
    GROUP BY WORKDEPT)

SELECT E.EMPNO,    E.LASTNAME,
    E.WORKDEPT,    E.SALARY,    X.DEPT_AVG_SAL
FROM EMPLOYEE E,
                X
WHERE E.WORKDEPT = X.WORKDEPT
ORDER BY E.WORKDEPT, E.SALARY
```

51. Take Advantage of REOPT Once:

This is a Bind option that controls DB2 to reoptimize an SQL statement during runtime when the statement is first received using the values placed in the host variables. It recalculates access path selection based on those values (as opposed to binding and optimizing with host variables), and then caches the access path chosen in the dynamic statement cache. This prevents each subsequent execution of an SQL statement in the package from getting reoptimize again on each execution of the statement. The Bind Option REOPT(VARS) will reoptimize an access path on every execution of every SQL statement.

Programs often receive values for a column or columns that have skewed data distribution. For example, an SQL statement may be executed based on a Status_Code value received, where one value for the Status_Code may represent up to 80% of the data in a table. The other values cover the other 20% of the data.

In these special cases, DB2 should reoptimize at runtime in order to see which value is being processed and allow the optimizer to select an access path accordingly.

continued …

REOPT Once cont...

NOTE: This is only helpful if there are frequency value runstat statistics generated on the Status_Code column. These statistics tell DB2 the different values in the table and the percentage of rows that meet those values. Without these special statistics, the REOPT will optimize no different than when it was bound using host variables.

In this example, the value with 80% of the data would be optimized to process the data via a tablespace scan, while all other values would have index processing as the chosen assess path.

There is some overhead involved in runtime optimization, but only when the reoptimization occurs many times during a run when using the REOPT(VARS). This is where the performance advantage comes in using REOPT(ONCE).

If the program is going to receive each value and open a cursor each time with that value, then the REOPT(VARS) would be needed. This ensures that on every open cursor, a reoptimization takes place for the new value. But keep in mind that with the REOPT(VARS), every other SQL statement that gets executed will also reoptimize each time. Depending on how many times SQL statements get executed during the run, all the reoptimization time can add up.

52. Identify Times for Volatile Tables:

The new VOLATILE table DDL key word identifies tables that are sometimes empty or have widely varying amounts of data. It specifies to the optimizer that index access should be used on this table whenever possible for SQL operations. However, be aware that list prefetch and certain other optimization techniques are disabled when VOLATILE is used. Many times developers have tables that get data deleted and reloaded for a process and the number of rows loaded in the table on each can vary greatly. This can be a problem since the tables need some data statistics, but the data varies. SAP and PeopleSoft applications frequently contain many tables like this and can be processed more efficiently with this enhancement. Also, ERP and CRM software packages with temporary work tables will perform better when this option is specified for those tables. To access these Volatile tables, the optimizer will use an index scan (rather than a table scan, regardless of the statistics) if that index is index-only (all referenced columns are in the index), or the index is able to apply a predicate in the index scan

If statistics are taken when the table is empty or has only a few rows, those statistics might not be appropriate when the table has many rows. Using the VOLATILE keyword on the CREATE or ALTER TABLE statement identifies tables whose data volumes fluctuate. The optimizer uses this keyword to decide to use an available index, if one exists. If the table is empty or contains only a small amount of data, there will be a slight performance penalty because the optimizer will use the index even if a table scan would have been better.

continued …

Volatile Tables cont...

For the many temporary tables used in PeopleSoft and SAP, this VOLATILE keyword should be added to those table definitions.

The VOLATILE table keyword is used as part of the Create Table DDL and the Alter Table DDL.

For Example:

```
Create Table Employee_Temp
 (Empno  Char(6)  Not Null,
  Lastname Varchar(15)  Not Null
  Volatile
 (
```

53. Use the ON COMMIT DROP enhancement.

This is a Declared Temporary Table improvement that causes declared temporary tables to be dropped automatically at commit. Use declared temporary tables when you need to store data for only the life of an application process and do not need to share the table definition. The definition of this table exists only while the application process runs. DB2 performs limited logging and locking operations for declared temporary tables. This enhancement is particularly important for distributed applications and stored procedures because clean up can occur when cursors are closed or commits occur.

```
DECLARE GLOBAL TEMPORARY TABLE
SESSION.EMP_TEMP1  (COL1 CHAR (20)
                    COL2 CHAR (10)
                    COL3 SNALLINT )
ON COMMIT DROP TABLE
```

Developers should consider coding this at all times when processing these declared tables. They also have other options which may increase performance at times if they are to reuse a table after some commit takes place.

ON COMMIT DELETE ROWS
ON COMMIT PRESERVE ROWS

54. Multiple Distincts:

As of V8, when applying the distinct word against specific columns, developers can get multiple distinct values back in one SQL statement. This is an automatic performance gain alleviating separate calls to DB2. For example:

Example 1:

```
SELECT SUM (DISTINCT SALARY),
        AVG(DISTINCT BONUS)
FROM EMPLOYEE;
```

Example 2:

```
SELECT COUNT(EMPNO)/COUNT(DISTINCT(WORKDEPT)),
        COUNT(DISTINCT(JOB))
FROM EMPLOYEE
```

55) Take Advantage of Backward Index Scan:

Version 8 of DB2 includes the capability for backward index scan. Backward index scan can improve performance of a SELECT statement with an ORDER BY *column* DESC clause because it reduces the need for DB2 to do sorts. In addition, the backward index scan capability can reduce the need for descending indexes because DB2 can now use ascending indexes to scan backward.

DB2 can use an index for a backward scan if the following conditions are true:

- The index is defined on the same columns as the columns in the ORDER BY clause, or the index is defined on the same columns as the columns in the ORDER BY clause, followed by other columns.
- For each column that is in the ORDER BY clause, the ordering that is specified in the index has to be the exact opposite of the ordering that is specified in the ORDER BY clause.

For plans or packages that were created in a previous release of DB2, you need to rebind the plans or packages for static SQL statements to take advantage of this enhancement.

56) Watch out for the Like statement.

The Like statement is an indexable stage 1 predicate when it is coded to check 'Begins with'. Know that the '%' or '_' at the beginning of the search string prevents DB2 from using a matching index and then causes either an index or tablespace scan.

Example 1: DB2 will not choose matching index processing for the following, even if an index exists for the column LASTNAME.

```
SELECT EMPNO, LASTNAME, SALARY
FROM EMPLOYEE
WHERE LASTNAME LIKE '%AND%'
```

Example 2: DB2 would choose matching index processing for the following:

```
SELECT EMPNO, LASTNAME, SALARY
FROM EMPLOYEE
WHERE LASTNAME LIKE 'AND%'
```

57) Set your clustering index correctly.

A *clustering index* determines how rows are physically ordered (clustered) in a table space. Clustering indexes provide significant performance advantages in some operations, particularly those that involve the retrieval of many rows. For example: Grouping and ordering operations and comparisons other than equal benefit from clustering indexes.

The order of data in a tablespace file is determined by one of the indexes being created with the 'Cluster=Yes' parameter. If no index is defined with this parameter, then by default it will be the first index created. More precisely it is the first index in the chain of indexes that is used in the database descriptor (which is typically the primary key index). When a tablespace Reorg utility is run, DB2 looks at the associated indexes for the one with the clustering parameter. The columns of this index determine the order of data put back into the tablespace file during the reorganization process.

1) It is very important to specify a clustering index based on your analysis of how the data is processed, especially in batch programs because they process the most data. Doing so minimizes the I/O 'Getpages' for better performance. Define the sequence of a clustering index to support the high-volume processing of data.

continued …

Clustering index cont...

2) One problem with allowing DB2 to default to a clustering index is that if indexes are ever dropped and recreated, the first index on the chain may not be the first index created anymore and another index may now become the clustering index on the next Reorg.

3) Organize the data in a tablespace according to the way the application typically processes. This will have a huge impact on performance, especially for those high-volume batch processes.

For Example: The Employee table is currently in EMPNO order starting with '000001' and ending in '999999'. But suppose most of the processing is by DEPTNO. Say there are numerous reports and screens that 'Group by DEPTNO', 'Order by DEPTNO', get averages and sums for DEPTNO, list employees by DEPTNO, etc. As these queries execute, there will be synchronous processing all over the tablespace file because the data is not in DEPTNO order. Take the following query:

SELECT EMPNO, LASTNAME, SALARY
FROM EMPLOYEE
WHERE DEPTNO = 'D11'

continued ...

Clustering index cont...

Employees that are part of 'D11' will be physically spread out all over the tablespace file because the data currently is in EMPNO order. This will cause many 'Getpage' request in order to retrieve the requested data. If there are 10 employees that are part of DEPTNO = 'D11', this could possible cause 10 'Getpage' requests.

But suppose the data were clustered by DEPTNO. In this case all 10 employees would probably be on the same datapage in the physical file, causing only one 'Getpage' request in order to retrieve the requested data. This just reduced the I/O on this query by 90%. So it is important to know your overall processing, especially batch, and get the data in the tablespace files in the correct order for processing.

58). Use Group By Expressions if Needed:

As of V8, DB2 now allows expressions in a 'Group By' clause. Prior to V8, if anything needed to be grouped by applying scalar functions, mathematics, concatenation, or anything special, the SQL had to create and materialize a nested table expression. Coding the expressions directly in the 'Group By' clause is more efficient. For Example: Provide a list of the number of employees for departments beginning with 'A', 'B', 'C', 'D', etc.

Old Way:

```
SELECT X.DEPT_GROUP, COUNT(*) AS #_EMPS
FROM
  (SELECT SUBSTR(WORKDEPT,1,1) AS DEPT_GROUP
   FROM EMPLOYEE) AS X
GROUP BY X.DEPT_GROUP
```

New Way:

```
SELECT SUBSTR(WORKDEPT,1,1) AS DEPT_GROUP
      ,COUNT(*) AS #_EMPS
FROM EMPLOYEE
GROUP BY SUBSTR(WORKDEPT,1,1)
```

59). Watch out for tablespace scans.

What do you do? If you as a developer see that a tablespace scan is occurring in your SQL execution, then go through the following checklist to help figure out why? Tablespace scans are a red flag and should always be researched. There are certain times when tablespaces scans are better than using indexes, but typically most queries should be using index processing through all the tables being processed.

If you go through this checklist, you should figure out why a tablespace scan has been chosen from the DB2 optimizer for its access path.

- The table could be small, and DB2 decides a tablespace scan may be faster than index processing.
- The catalog statistics say the table is small, or maybe there are no statistics on the table.
- The predicates are such that DB2 thinks the query is going to retrieve a large enough amount of data that would require a tablespace scan.
- The predicates are such that DB2 picks a non-clustered index, and the number of pages to retrieve is high enough based on total number of pages in the table to require a tablespace scan.
- The tablespace file or index files could physically be out of shape and need a REORG.
- The predicates in the query do not match any available indexes on the table.
- The predicate(s) may be poorly coded in a non-indexable way.

94

60) Do not ask for what you already know.

This might sound obvious, but most programmers violate this rule at one time or another. For example:

SELECT EMPNO, LASTNAME, SALARY
FROM EMPLOYEE
WHERE EMPNO = '000010'

The problem is that EMPNO is included in the select list. You already know that EMPNO will be equal to the value '000010' because that is what the WHERE clause tells DB2 to do. But with EMPNO listed in the WHERE clause, DB2 will dutifully retrieve that column, too. This slows performance.

61). Order of Tables in a Query:

It does not matter the order of tables coded when coding Inner joins. DB2 allows it optimizer to choose what it thinks is the most efficient order of tables to process through. The optimizer will choose the order of tables based on the predicates being applied to each table. The table that the optimizer thinks will be filtered the most is chosen as the starting table, which minimizes the I/O to the other tables. Pay special attention to this when looking at performance. The DB2 Explain tool will show the order of tables the optimizer has chosen to process through for any particular query.

When coding outer joins, the developer needs to only make sure they have the correct starting table, sometimes called the 'Driver' table. This is the starting point for DB2 to branch out and execute all outer join logic to the other tables in the query. The order of all the other tables being outer joined to does not matter.

Example 1: Department table will be the starting (driver) table in this statement:

```
SELECT D.DEPTNO, D.DEPTNAME, D.MGRNO,
        E.LASTNAME, P.PROJNO, P.PROJNAME
FROM DEPARTMENT  D LEFT JOIN
        EMPLOYEE    E  ON D.MGRNO = E.EMPNO
                        LEFT JOIN
        PROJECT      P  ON P.DEPTNO = D.DEPTNO
```

Order of Tables cont...

Is the same logic as:

```
SELECT D.DEPTNO, D.DEPTNAME, D.MGRNO,
        E.LASTNAME, P.PROJNO, P.PROJNAME
FROM DEPARTMENT  D LEFT JOIN
      PROJECT       P  ON P.DEPTNO = D.DEPTNO
                       LEFT JOIN
      EMPLOYEE      E  ON D.MGRNO = E.EMPNO
```

Example 2: Department table will be the starting (driver) table in this statement:

```
SELECT D.DEPTNO, D.DEPTNAME, D.MGRNO,
        E.LASTNAME
FROM EMPLOYEE      E  RIGHT JOIN
      DEPARTMENT  D  ON D.MGRNO = E.EMPNO
                       RIGHT JOIN
      PROJECT       P  ON P.DEPTNO = D.DEPTNO
```

Order of Tables cont...

Is the same logic as:

SELECT D.DEPTNO, D.DEPTNAME, D.MGRNO,
       E.LASTNAME
FROM PROJECT   P RIGHT JOIN
     DEPARTMENT **D** ON D.DEPTNO = P.DEPTNO
                   RIGHT JOIN
     EMPLOYEE   E ON E.EMPNO = D.MGRNO

Note: What is important here throughout these examples is the starting table with outer joins. The order of the other 2 tables in the SQL statement being left joined to do not matter.

62). Use Left Outer Joins over Right Outer Joins:

When coding outer join logic, it does not matter whether the developer codes a 'Left Outer Join' or a 'Right Outer Join' in order to get the logic correct, as long as they have the starting 'Driver' table coded correctly. See the tuning tip #61 on 'Order of Tables in a Query'. There is no difference between a Left and Right outer join other than where the starting 'Driver' is coded. For example the following 2 queries are identical:

Example 1: Department table will be the starting (driver) table:

```
SELECT D.DEPTNO, D.DEPTNAME, D.MGRNO,
        E.LASTNAME
FROM DEPARTMENT  D LEFT JOIN
        EMPLOYEE    E  ON D.MGRNO = E.EMPNO
```

Example 2: Department table will also be the starting (driver) table:

```
SELECT D.DEPTNO, D.DEPTNAME, D.MGRNO,
        E.LASTNAME
FROM  EMPLOYEE       E  RIGHT JOIN
        DEPARTMENT  D  ON D.MGRNO = E.EMPNO
```

continued ...

Use Left over Right Outer Joins cont...

Whichever table is to the left of 'Left Outer Join' is the starting 'Driver' table. Also whichever table is to the right of 'Right Outer Join' is the starting 'Driver' table.

The interesting part of these examples is that the DB2 optimizer actually takes any 'Right Outer Join' queries and rewrites them to 'Left Outer Join' queries before executing. This can be seen in the DB2 Explain tool by looking at the JOIN_TYPE column in the Explain.

Left versus Right Outer Joins can be confusing to many developers that may not know the specifics of each. This leads to confusion when many queries in an application are coded with 'Left Outer Joins' and many others are coded with 'Right Outer Joins'. It can be even more confusing when in the same query, there are both 'Left' and 'Right' outer joins between tables.

Developers in DB2 should only code 'Left Outer Joins'. It is more straight forward because the starting 'Driver' table is always coded first, and all subsequent tables being joined to have 'Left Outer Join' coded beside them, making it more understandable and readable.

63). Checking for Non Existence:

When coding logic to determine what rows in a table do not exists in another table, there are a couple of common approaches. One approach is to code outer join logic and then check 'Where COLB IS NULL' from the other table, or coding 'Not Exists' logic. The following 2 examples both bring back employees that are not managers on the department table.

Example 1:

```
SELECT E.EMPNO, E.LASTNAME
FROM EMPLOYEE     E  LEFT JOIN
        DEPARTMENT D  ON D.MGRNO = E.EMPNO
WHERE D.MGRNO IS NULL
```

Example 2:
```
SELECT E.EMPNO, E.LASTNAME
FROM EMPLOYEE  E
WHERE NOT EXISTS
   (SELECT 1
    FROM DEPARTMENT D
    WHERE D.MGRNO = E.EMPNO)
```

continued ...

Checking for Non Existence cont...

Both approaches are logically equivalent, but perform very differently. The second approach with the 'Not Exists' will perform much more efficiently. When coding for exceptions in outer join logic, the predicate 'WHERE D.MGRNO IS NULL' will not be applied until after the join process takes place. This causes the result set to be built with both the rows that are managers and the rows that are not managers, only to eliminate the managers after the joining. The second approach will execute its filtering during processing and only write out to the result set those non managers. This difference in processing, depending on the amount of data being processed can have a huge impact on performance.

64). Stored Procedures:

Stored Procedures are programs running in the database environment. They can be written in SQL, C, Java, Cobol, etc. and help to reduce the network traffic. In any case, stored procedures are typically written to contain multiple SQL data manipulation language (DML) statements as well as procedure logic constructs such as loops and if/else statements. Therefore, stored procedures are conceptually similar to "small" programs, providing useful, database-intensive business services to multiple applications. Many applications, which some are remote from the DBMS itself, invoke the stored procedure with a single SQL call statement.

Stored procedures can require parameters for input (IN), output (OUT), or input and output (INOUT). They may also return one or more sets of results.

Keep in mind that calling a SP has an overhead and it should be clear that it makes no sense to have a single statement inside the SP. The benefit arises if the network traffic reduces significantly. This can be the case if the SP includes several SQL statements, or has loops executing SQL statements.

continued ...

Stores Procedures cont...

If a stored procedure is necessary, consider the use of native SQL procedures for even better efficiency. An external stored procedure with SQL needs a complete language environment for the user program, and then that external program comes back to get its package loaded, assignment of Task Control Blocks and SQL statements executed. When an incoming stored procedure request is queued for the Work Load Managers, the DB2 thread may be suspended for a time.

With native SQL procedures, the thread will just switch packages when the call statement is processed and run the procedure - no queuing. The storage used for the local variables is above the bar and managed with efficient algorithms.

65). Do not select a column in order to sort on it.

DB2 no longer requires selection of a column simply to do a sort. Therefore in this example, D.LOCATION does not require selection if the end user does not need that value. Remove items from the SELECT list to prevent unnecessary processing. It is no longer required to SELECT columns used in the ORDER BY or GROUP BY clauses. For Example:

```
SELECT D.DEPTNO, D.DEPTNAME, E.LASTNAME
FROM DEPARTMENT  D  LEFT JOIN
     EMPLOYEE      E  ON D.MGRNO = E.EMPNO
WHERE D.DEPTNO IN (:HV-DEPTNO1,
                       :HV-DEPTNO2)
ORDER BY D.LOCATION, D.DEPTNO
```

As can be seen in this SQL statement, the D.LOCATION is being sorted on but is not part of the select clause.

66). Always limit the result set if possible.

FETCH FIRST n ROWS ONLY.

The FETCH FIRST n ROWS ONLY clause should be used if there are a known, maximum number of rows that will be FETCHed from a result set. This clause limits the number of rows returned from a result set by invoking a fast implicit close. Pages are quickly released in the buffer pool when the nth result row has been processed.

Do not confuse this with the OPTIMIZE FOR n ROWS clause. That clause does not invoke a fast implicit close and will keep locking and fetching until the cursor is implicitly or explicitly closed by the developer. In contrast, FETCH FIRST n ROWS ONLY will not allow the n+1 row to be FETCHed and results in an SQLCODE = +100.

67). Take advantage of DB2 V8 enhanced DISCARD capabilities when it comes to mass deletes.

Many times, programs need to periodically delete a significant number of rows in a table. This could be a weekly, monthly, quarterly, or yearly job that typically gets scheduled on a certain day and time in order to minimize concurrency issues. Developers try their best to minimize these issues by declaring cursors 'With Hold', and executing frequent commits. This helps, but there is also a logging issue with DB2 that can affect performance. For programs deleting hundreds of thousands, or millions of rows, the DB2 logs can begin to fill up which can causes the OLTP transactions and batch processes to suffer.

Take advantage of the V8 DISCARD capabilities for this example and have the DBAs set up a REORG with SHRLEVEL CHANGE (also called ONLINE REORG). This ONLINE REORG allows others to have read and write access to the data while it unloads and reloads the data currently in the table. Using the DISCARD function with the REORG specifies the rows to be removed when unloading, and places them into a discard file.

Notes: Make sure 'LOG NO' is specified as a REORG parameter. If by chance one of the rows being discarded happened to have been updated by another process during the REORG time, the REORG job will terminate with a return code of 8.

See the IBM DB2 Manuals for more specific information pertaining to ONLINE REORGs.

68). Take advantage of the DB2 LOAD utility for mass inserts.

Many times, programs need to periodically insert a significant number of rows in a table. For the best performance, these records to be inserted should be written out to a file, and have a DB2 LOAD utility load the records into the table using the file. This is generally more efficient than a program   Load formats data pages directly, while avoiding most of the overhead of individual row processing that inserts incur (for example, logging is virtually eliminated). Also, load utilities can better exploit parallelism on multiprocessor machines.

The LOAD utility is used to batch load data into DB2 tables. During this process LOAD performs all necessary data conversions (e.g., character to date format) and error processing (e.g., rejecting records with duplicate keys). Discarded input records are written to a sequential file, which can subsequently be examined to determine the reason or reasons for rejection. The LOAD utility will always produce a return code of at least '04' because a COPY is required following a LOAD.

69). Watch out for Materialization of Views, Nested Table Expressions and Common table Expressions.

Sometimes these expressions will be merged into the query by the DB2 optimizer without executing and materializing the data first. Typically if the expression has a Group By, Distinct or Union the expression will get materialized in a work file table. When this materialization occurs, overhead is incurred in the creating and loading of this work file, and many times this work file table is then joined to other tables. This can be troublesome due the fact that the materialized table contains no indexes. If the program or query contains views or expressions, then execute a DB2 explain. If the name of the view or expression shows up in the DB2 explain output as a table name, then materialization is taking place by DB2. A possibility for tuning is to make the materialized output into a base table for processing, and then reference the base table in place of the view or expression. Other times, if the output is aggregated data, the query can be rewritten with a scalar fullselect (see tuning tip #50). Another possibility is to make the table into a Global Temporary Table and define an index for the materialized data (see tuning tip #13).

In the following examples, if the view name EMP_VIEW1, the nested expression name E1, or the common expression name DEPT_SAL_TABLE show up in the DB2 explain output, then materialization is taking place.

continued ...

Materialization of Views and Expressions cont...

Example 1 View:

```
CREATE VIEW EMP_VIEW1 AS
  SELECT WORKDEPT, AVG(SALARY) AS AVG_SAL
  FROM EMPLOYEE
  GROUP BY WORKDEPT
;
SELECT     E.EMPNO,     E.SALARY,     E.WORKDEPT,
E1.AVG_SAL
FROM EMPLOYEE E,
  EMP_VIEW1   E1
WHERE E.WORKDEPT = E1.WORKDEPT
ORDER BY E.WORKDEPT, E.EMPNO
;
```

Example 2 Nested Table Expression:

```
SELECT E.EMPNO, E.SALARY, E.WORKDEPT, E1.AVG_SAL
FROM EMPLOYEE E,
  (SELECT WORKDEPT, AVG(SALARY) AS AVG_SAL
   FROM EMPLOYEE
   GROUP BY WORKDEPT) AS E1
WHERE E.WORKDEPT = E1.WORKDEPT
ORDER BY E.WORKDEPT, E.EMPNO
;
```

continued ...

Materialization of Views and Expressions cont...

Example 3 Common Table Expression:

```
WITH DEPT_SAL_TABLE  AS
 (SELECT WORKDEPT, AVG(SALARY) AS AVG_SAL
  FROM EMPLOYEE
  GROUP BY WORKDEPT)

SELECT     E.EMPNO,     E.SALARY,     E.WORKDEPT,
E1.AVG_SAL
FROM EMPLOYEE      E,
   DEPT_SAL_TABLE E1
WHERE E.WORKDEPT = E1.WORKDEPT
ORDER BY E.WORKDEPT, E.EMPNO
;
```

Example 4 Scalar Fullselect:

The following rewrite using a scalar fullselect yields the same result, and will not have materialization because the average salary gets calculated during the processing.

```
SELECT E.EMPNO, E.SALARY, E.WORKDEPT,
     (SELECT  AVG(SALARY)
      FROM EMPLOYEE E2
      WHERE E.WORKDEPT
          = E2.WORKDEPT) AS AVG_SAL
FROM EMPLOYEE    E
ORDER BY E.WORKDEPT, E.EMPNO
;
```

70). Consider Compressing Data.

DBAs can compress data in a table space or partition by specifying COMPRESS YES on CREATE TABLESPACE or ALTER TABLESPACE and then running the LOAD or REORG utility. In many cases, using the COMPRESS clause can significantly reduce the amount of disk space needed to store data, but the compression ratio you achieve depends on the characteristics of your data. This can actually increase the number of rows on each page of data, which can then reduce the amount of I/O when retrieving data. There is some processing overhead required when the data is stored and when the data is retrieved from storage. The decompressing overhead is much less than the compressing of data when it is loaded or inserted. Compression may allow applications or queries to see significant gains in performance depending on the amount of compression accomplished on table data. Some of what an application sees with compressed data is:

- Higher buffer pool hit rations. Having more rows per page allows for more data to stay in the buffer pools.
- Fewer I/Os
- Fewer getpage operations
- More efficient logging. Data that is logged because of SQL changes is compressed. Thus, applications can expect less logging for insertions and deletions but the amount of logging for updates varies.

continued …

Compressing Data cont...

There is a DSN1COMP utility that will estimate how well data will compress for a specific table.

In some cases, especially for data that is heavily updated, using compressed data results in an increase in the number of getpage request, lock request, and synchronous read I/Os. If the pages of data for a table contain compressed fixed-length rows with little or no free space, any updated rows probably will get stored in an overflow page. This can be offset by increasing the free space of the pages.

71). Consider Parallelism.

When DB2 plans to access data from a table or index in a partitioned table space, it can initiate multiple parallel operations. The response time for data or processor-intensive queries can be significantly reduced. Most shops in an IBM Z/OS environment have a computer containing multiple processors. You can significantly reduce the response time for data or processor-intensive queries by taking advantage of the ability of DB2 to initiate multiple parallel operations when it accesses data from a table or index in a partitioned table space. Queries cannot take advantage of parallelism unless you enable parallel processing. To enable:

For static SQL, specify DEGREE(ANY) on BIND or REBIND

For dynamic SQL, execute SET CURRENT DEGREE='ANY'

Parallel operations usually involve at least one table in a partitioned table space. Scans of large partitioned table spaces have the greatest performance improvements where both I/O and central processor (CP) operations can be carried out in parallel. But both partitioned and non partitioned tables can take advantage of parallelism.

There are many shops on V8 that bind everything into production for parallelism, and there are some shops that seem reluctant to do so because if controls are not in place, a program can begin consuming all the available resources from each of the CPU processors. Most programs will perform faster in parallelism mode, especially those jobs that consume large amounts of data. See your DBAs for assistance.

72). Keep STDDEV, STDDEV_SAMP, VAR, VAR_SAMP functions apart from other functions

When DB2 executes queries containing aggregate functions, many of these functions can be evaluated when the data is retrieved rather than afterward. These four aggregate functions are always evaluated late after the data retrieval. The more simple aggregate functions like Min, Max, Sum, Avg and Count are many times evaluated during the data retrieval process, unless they are included with one of these four.

73). Consider Direct Row Access using ROWID datatype.

If a column in a table is defined as a ROWID datatype, the ROWID value implicitly contains the location of the row. If the ROWID value is then used in the search condition of subsequent update or deletes, then DB2 may navigate directly to the row, bypassing any index processing or tablespace scans. This direct row accessing is very fast. In order to take advantage of it, the ROWID value must first be selected into a host variable and then referenced on subsequent update or delete statements. This would be recommended if rows were already being selected before any updates or deletes took place. For example, if a customer needs to change an order, the order information is typically retrieved first , reviewed, and then updates or deletes take place. Replacing current update or delete processes that do not have a need to select the data first would not be candidates. For example:

```
CREATE TABLE EMPLOYEE
  (EMPNO    CHAR(6)  NOT NULL,
   EMP_ID   ROWID    NOT NULL
                     GENERATED ALWAYS,
   LASTNAME CHAR(25) NOT NULL,
   ....
   .... )
```

continued ...

ROWID cont...

```
SELECT EMP_ID, LASTNAME, ...
INTO :HV-EMPID-ROWID-VALUE,
      :HV-LASTNAME
FROM EMPLOYEE
WHERE EMPNO = '000010'

UPDATE EMPLOYEE
SET SALARY = SALARY * 1.1
WHERE EMPID = :HV-EMPID-ROWID-VALUE
```

NOTES:
1) For COBOL Applications the datatype in working storage is

```
    10 EMP-ID      USAGE SQL TYPE IS ROWID
```

2) For others the declared variable is

```
    EXEC SQL BEGIN DECLARE SECTION;
    SQL TYPE is ROWID HV-EMPID-ROWID-VALUE;
    SHORT         HV-EMPNO;
    CHAR          HV-LASTNAME[30];
    DECIMAL(7,2)  HV-SALARY;
    EXEC SQL END DECLARE SECTION;
```

continued ...

ROWID cont…

3) Although DB2 might plan to use direct row access, circumstances can cause DB2 to not use direct row access at run time. That circumstance is the possibility of the row being moved before the update or delete takes place. The only way this could happen is due to a DB2 REORG or another process deleting and re-inserting the row.

4) Write your applications to handle the possibility that direct row access might not be used by also including a key value in the SQL statement. If an index exists on EMPNO, DB2 can use index access if direct access fails.

```
UPDATE EMPLOYEE
SET SALARY = SALARY * 1.1
WHERE EMPID = :HV-EMPID-ROWID-VALUE
    AND EMPNO = '000010'
```

5) See the IBM manuals for further detail.

74). Test your queries with realistic statistics, and a level of data to reflect performance issues.

Most organizations have at least three database environments: development, test, and production. Programmers use the development database environment to create and test applications, which are then more rigorously examined in the test environment by programmers and users before they are migrated to the production environment.

When a SQL statement or program is being tested in a test or QA environment, try to make sure the test database contains data that reflects the production database. An SQL statement tested with unrealistic data may behave differently when used in production. To ensure rigorous testing, the data distribution in the test environment should closely resemble that in the production environment. Many shops do not have the luxury of copying production data to a test environment due to the size of many tables. These shops offset this issue by copying production data statistics from the system catalog tables (Systables, Syscolumns, Syscoldist, Sysindexes, etc.). By having test tables at least reflecting the same 'Runstat' information, any SQL or program should then create an access path during Bind/Prepare optimization that will reflect production when it gets migrated. This is a pretty good alternative except for those times when the access path looks good, yet the query or program runs longer than it should.

continued …

Test your queries with realistic statistics cont...

There should always be some level of data in a test environment to reflect poor performance even when the Explain access path looks good. For example, a program's optimization may show a good access path and run in 10 minutes. But 10 minutes may be way too long for processing tables that may have only a few hundred thousand rows. This runtime would then be more exaggerated when it gets migrated and executed in production. This is exactly why developers should always display processing counts at the end of their programs so it can be shown exactly how much processing and I/O took place during its execution. They can then compare these numbers to runtime and CPU time to figure out if their program actually ran efficiently or not.

75). Specify the leading index columns in WHERE clauses

For a composite index, the following query would use the index and execute matching processing as long as the leading column of the index is specified in the WHERE clause.
Index = (Part_Num, Product_Num)

```
SELECT *
FROM PARTS_TABLE
WHERE PART_NUM = 100;
```

Whereas the next query would *not* use the composite index as a matching index, but the optimizer may still choose to use the index in its processing, but would have to execute a index file scan.

```
SELECT *
FROM PARTS_TABLE
WHERE PRODUCT_ID = 5555;
```

continued ...

Specify the leading index columns cont...

Many developers rewrite queries like the following thinking that DB2 will then take advantage of the index by applying a predicate on the first column of the index that actually does no filtering. In this query, it is assumed that the PART_NUM column will always have a value greater than zero. The explain for this statement may look better because it may show a matching index process, but in actuality, the processing will be no different than the previous index scan due to the fact that the first predicate really does no filtering and DB2 must still scan through the index and look at every entry. This would be the same processing as the index scan. Index scans show up in DB2 Explains as 'Index Processing', but zero matching columns.

```
SELECT *
FROM PARTS
WHERE PART_NUM > 0
AND PRODUCT_ID = 5555;
```

76). Use WHERE instead of HAVING for record filtering whenever possible.

Avoid using the HAVING clause along with GROUP BY to filter data if at all possible. Sometimes rows can be excluded with just the WHERE clause in place of coding the HAVING clause. The Having clause is to filter groups after the 'Group By' processing has taken place, and the Where clause filter data during processing. The first statement causes DB2 to gather up all the different DEPTID values using a sort to group them, and then eliminate all groups but the DEPTID = 100. This becomes a two step process with a sort for DB2, whereas the second query will only gather up the data specific to DEPTNO = 100 and sum their salaries. This eliminates much sort and I/O time.

For Example:

SELECT DEPTID,
SUM(SALARY)
FROM EMP
GROUP BY DEPTID
HAVING DEPTID = 100;

However, the same query can be rewritten to exploit the index and eliminate all other groupings cutting down on sort time.

SELECT DEPTID,
SUM(SALARY)
FROM EMP
WHERE DEPTID = 100

77). Keep in mind 'Index Only' processing whenever possible.

Many times, developers are coding queries that need to execute one of the four column aggregate functions (Sum, Avg, Min, Max) and can get some great results by including an extra column as part of an index. Take for example the following query and associated index. Index1 = (YEAR, PERIOD, LEDGER_ID).

SELECT SUM(JRNL_AMT)
FROM LEDGER_TABLE
WHERE YEAR = 2008
    AND PERIOD IN (1,2,3)

This query will optimize matching 2 columns (Year and Period) on Index1, but the processing must then go to the tablespace file to gather all the pages of data that meet the criteria in order to sum up the JRNL_AMT column. This at times can cause a lot of I/O between the index file and data file. Often times in financial processing there are amounts that get totaled up by month, quarter and year. If this is a query that gets executed often for varying Year and Period ranges only to sum up 1 column = JRNL_AMT, the way to tune and get this query to execute faster is to add the JRNL_AMT column to Index1. That index would now be (YEAR, PERIOD, LEDGER_ID, JRNL_AMT).

continued …

Keep in mind 'Index Only' processing cont...

DB2 is good at recognizing this JRNL_AMT column in the index, even though there is no specific predicate on it, and will choose 'Index Only' processing. All of the I/O costs that DB2 previously incurred in going to the tablespace file to get the JNRL_AMTs has been eliminated. This will be a huge savings in performance, significantly improving response time. This does not mean to overload all index files with extra columns to try and get all processes to optimize as 'Index Only', but there are special times where it makes sense. If the column JRNL_AMT is a heavily updated column, then this may not be a good solution for faster response times. The updating of columns that are part of an index incurs a lot of index processing overhead.

CHAPTER 2: DB2 SQL HINTS

Every RDMS has what are called 'Hints' to code in SQL statements to try to get the optimizer to choose something different in its optimization. Examples of choosing something different would be to direct DB2 to choose a different index, a different order of the table flow, or a different join method. These hints are to be used when the access path for an SQL statement does not perform very well, and all other options have been exhausted, such as:

- Rewriting the query a different way
- Hard coding versus host variables
- Reorgs of the table and index files
- Runstats for the tables involved
- Frequency Value Runstats for specific columns involved
- Redesign of any appropriate indexes
- Rewriting predicates, yet keeping the same logic

The DB2 optimizer is very good at picking the correct access path for an SQL statement, and continues to get better in every DB2 release. But it can never be perfect. That is why at times SQL coding tricks or hints should be added to an SQL statement. Typically if DB2 chooses an access path that is not performing well, then statistics on the columns involved in the predicates should be looked at first, then the predicate itself, to see if 'REOPT ONCE' is needed at runtime. But there are other statements that can help also as a last resort.

1) Add 'Optimize for 1 Row' statement at the very end of the SQL statement.

This statement is *not* to be added to every coded SQL statement. It is to be used only when tuning a query that is not performing well. If an SQL statement has been Explained, and the Explain output looks good yet performance is still an issue, then this statement *may* make it perform better by getting it to optimize differently.

This statement tells the optimizer that the SQL's intent may be to only retrieve a small subset of the whole result set, and to give higher priority to the retrieval of the first row. By coding this statement, the optimizer *may* at times choose to:

- Eliminate some sorts (especially join sorts). The optimizer will try to choose an access path that will avoid sorts. If a value other than 1 Row is specified, DB2 may choose an access path based on cost, and won't necessarily avoid sorts.

- Eliminate List Prefetch. Prefetch is kicked in by the optimizer to minimize the number of 'Getpages' that DB2 has to perform in order to retrieve all the data requested for a specific table. But in order to minimize the 'Getpages', DB2 must first execute a RID sort. There are times where more 'Getpages' without a RID sort may perform better than fewer 'Getpages' with a RID sort.

continued ...

Optimize for 1 Row cont...

Additional Notes:

- This statement does not prevent DB2 from retrieving all of the qualified rows, nor does it prevent the application program or query from returning all qualified rows in the result set.

- This statement will not always improve performance. By adding it to a statement, it could add to the total elapsed time in retrieving all the qualifying rows. But for queries that are currently not performing well, it is worth trying.

- This statement is only effective on queries for which DB2 can build the result set incrementally. Any queries that require some kind of sort of the final result set will not be affected. For example, most queries that use Distinct, Group By, Order By, or Union may not see any changes with this statement.

- Many OLTP applications code every query with 'Optimize for 1 Row' because in most queries it will eliminate the List Prefetch. The List Prefetch gets executed by the optimizer in order to minimize the number of 'Getpages'. But most OLTP queries do not retrieve much data, thus already executing very few 'Getpages'. By eliminating the List Prefetch, DB2 is eliminating the creating of a sort work file, the loading of the small amount of data into it, and the sorting. This is all overhead which will make the OLTP response time a little faster.

2). **Add the A.PKEY = A.PKEY predicate to the SQL query, where PKEY equals the primary key column of the table.**

This statement is **_not_** to be added to every coded SQL statement. It is to be used only when tuning a query that is not performing well. Again, this is not a guarantee that a query will execute better, only that it may get the optimizer to choose a different access path, which could possibly make it perform better.

With queries that involve multiple table joins, the order in which the tables are processed is of extreme importance when it comes to performance. There are times when DB2 may choose an order of tables that may not be optimal. We want DB2 to choose the table that will have the least number of rows returned after its predicates are applied. To ensure a specific table is processed first in a multi table join, code the A.PKEY =A.PKEY. For Example:

```
SELECT E.EMPNO, E.LASTNAME
FROM EMPLOYEE      E,
       DEPARTMENT D
WHERE D.DEPTNO IN ('A00', 'C11', 'D21)
    AND E.SALARY > 50000.00
    AND E.JOB IN ('MANAGER', 'PROGRAMMER')
    AND D.MGRNO = E.EMPNO
```

continued …

A.PKEY = A.PKEY predicate cont...

If DB2 chose to begin with the DEPT table as the starting table, and we want to see what would happen if DB2 chose to start at the EMP table, we would then code:

```
SELECT E.EMPNO, E.LASTNAME
FROM EMPLOYEE   E,
        DSN87610.DEPT D
WHERE D.DEPTNO IN ('A00', 'C11', 'D21)
    AND E.SALARY > 50000.00
    AND E.JOB IN ('MANAGER', 'PROGRAMMER')
    AND D.MGRNO = E.EMPNO
    AND E.EMPNO = E.EMPNO
```

Additional Notes:

- This statement does not always change the order of tables, but many times will.

-      This statement often times changes the join type between tables. Changing the join type may then have an affect on index choices, List Prefetch, sorts, etc. If the optimization has chosen a merge scan or hybrid join, then by adding this statement typically changes it to a nested loop join. Again keep in kind that this does not mean that changing the chosen optimization will make it perform better, only that it may get the optimizer to choose a different access path, which could possibly make it perform better.

3). Disqualify an index choice.

Sometimes the optimizer may have multiple indexes to choose from when figuring out an access path. It is very good at choosing the one or ones that will provide the best performance. But in cases where performance is not so good, and we want to get the optimizer to choose another index to see if it runs better, and then consider the following:

```
SELECT EMPNO, LASTNAME, HIREDATE
FROM EMPLOYEE
WHERE EMPNO BETWEEN :WS-FIRST-EMPNO
                AND :WS_LAST_EMPNO
    AND  LASTNAME LIKE 'H%'
    AND WORKDEPT IN(:WS-DEPT1, :WS-DEPT2,
                                :WS-DEPT3)
```

There exists an index on each of the columns coded.
Index1 on Empno
Index2 on Lastname
Index3 on Workdept

The optimizer may choose to:

- Use the index on EMPNO to get those rows, and then compare them to the other predicates
- Use the index on LASTNAME to get those rows, and then compare them to the other predicates
- Use the index on WORKDEPT to get those rows, and then compare them to the other predicates
- Use a combination of multiple predicate index access

Disqualify an index choice cont...

Suppose the optimizer chose to use the index for EMPNO, but that predicate gets more rows than the other 2 predicates. To get the optimizer to choose one of the other indexes, we make the EMPNO predicate a non-indexable predicate by applying some SQL scalar function to it. For Example:

```
SELECT EMPNO, LASTNAME, HIREDATE
 FROM EMPLOYEE
WHERE RTRIM(EMPNO) BETWEEN :WS-FIRST-EMPNO
                       AND :WS_LAST_EMPNO
   AND  LASTNAME LIKE 'H%'
   AND WORKDEPT IN(:WS-DEPT1, :WS-DEPT2,
                            :WS-DEPT3)
```

Coded this way, the optimizer definitely will not choose the EMPNO index, and now is forced to choose one of the other indexes which may execute much faster.

continued ...

Disqualifying an index choice cont...

Anytime the optimizer sees anything being done to a column in a predicate, it automatically makes it a non-indexable predicate. If the column is a character string, then any of the character Scalar functions will work. If the column is a numeric, then apply any of the numeric Scalar functions, or add +0 to it. For example:

WHERE DEC(SALARY,7,2) > 50000.00 making it a
   non-indexable predicate

WHERE SALARY + 0 > 50000.00 making it a
   non-indexable predicate.

If it's a Date column, then just code:

WHERE DATE(HIREDATE) > '2005-01-01' making it a
   non-indexable column.

Note: It is always best to first pay attention to the statistics on the columns involved in the predicates and try to figure out why DB2 chose the index that it did. Its choice will be based on calculated filter factors for predicates involved. Typically there is a predicate that DB2 does not have much information on and gets the calculated filter factor incorrect based on the values coming in at runtime. If time allows, try to figure this out before recoding a predicate as non indexable.

4). Changing the order of table processing

How we physically code the order of tables in Inner Join processing does not dictate the order by which the optimizer will choose to process through the tables.

Let's assume Tables A, B, and C each has indexes on columns C1, C2, C3, and C4.

Sometimes DB2 underestimates the number of rows that will be retrieved based on predicates coded on each table. Typically we want DB2 to choose as the starting table the one table that will have the fewest rows returned, thus reducing I/O as it joins to the other tables.

If DB2 underestimates the number of rows selected from table A and wrongly chooses that as the first table in the join,

a) you can reduce the estimated size of Table A by adding more predicates,

or

b) disfavor any index on the join column by making the join predicate on table A nonindexable.

continued ...

Changing the order of table processing cont...

Example: The following query illustrates option b.

```
SELECT * FROM T1 A, T1 B, T1 C
WHERE (A.C1 = B.C1 OR 0=1)
    AND A.C2 = C.C2
    AND A.C2 BETWEEN :HV1 AND :HV2
    AND A.C3 BETWEEN :HV3 AND :HV4
    AND A.C4 < :HV5
    AND B.C2 BETWEEN :HV6 AND :HV7
    AND B.C3 < :HV8
    AND C.C2 < :HV9;
```

The result of making the join predicate between A and B a non indexable predicate (which cannot be used in single index access) disfavors the use of the index on column C1. This, in turn, might lead DB2 to access table A or B first. Or, it might lead DB2 to change the access type of table A or B, thereby influencing the join sequence of the other tables. Adding the 'OR 0=1' is another way to make an existing predicate non indexable.

CHAPTER 3: SQL STANDARDS AND GUIDELINES

Every IT shop that has applications involving DB2 should have a set of SQL standards and guidelines for their developers to follow. This chapter is a start for developers and project managers to use as part of their development. Once you have a set of standards and guidelines, be sure to enforce them. Every program should have code walkthroughs to ensure that standards and guidelines are being followed.

The list that follows serves two purposes. One relates to performance, and the other serves to alleviate abends and/or production incident reporting.

The list is broke out into 2 separate areas. One specific to Cobol SQL developers and the other are specific for all SQL developers (no matter the language in which they are embedding their SQL code).

FOR COBOL PROGRAMS:

1) The SQLCODE must be checked after every SQL statement. The Declare cursor statement is only a declarative, and gets no return code from DB2. All other SQL calls will get some return code. Return code data from the DB2 database system gets automatically loaded in the SQLCA communications area.

2) Every program must include the SQLCA and a DCLGEN for each table being coded against. The DCLGEN is predefined with host variables that match the column definitions. They are used to select data into, insert and update from, and serve as the host variables in any 'Where' statement.

If DCLGEN fields are not being used, then any program declaring variables in the code must make sure that the variable being declared matches EXACTLY the definition in DB2. If it doesn't, then there is a likelihood DB2 may not choose an index to process. For example if Column1 is defined as an Integer, then the host variable in Cobol should be defined as S9(9) comp.

3) Every program must have a consistent DB2 abend routine. For batch programs, it is easiest to have a called program that handles the displaying of the SQLCA fields, and calls the 'DSNTIAR' DB2 routine to display further DB2 messages. For online programs, sometimes it is good to write out the SQLCA and DSNTIAR information to a file or table in order to fall back on errors that occur. Make sure the SQLSTATE is displayed out along with the SQLCODE.

4) Never code 'Select *' in a program. Only code for the columns needed. If a program needs all the columns, then code each one. This will prevent an abend if there is ever a new column added to the table. The fewer columns being brought into the program, the more efficient the processing (see tuning tip #3 and tuning tip #29). More columns can have an effect on performance due to larger sort sizes, possible index-only processing, and join types. When DB2 looks at which join type is best, part of its analysis is the number of columns from each table being selected.

5) Make sure any columns defined as 'Nullable' contain a null indicator host variable as part of the select, insert, or update statements. This is most important in select statements because DB2 will return an invalid -305 SQLCODE when it returns a column of null to the program, and there is no null indicator specified. These null indicators must be defined in working storage as Pic S9(4) Comp.

It is preferable to code the Value, Coalesce, or Ifnull SQL scalar function for any nullable columns because the program will not receive null indicators from DB2. This will alleviate -305 SQL errors where a program is not set up to handle the null indicator. It will also spare the program from having to define the null indicators in Working Storage.

For example:

Select COALESCE(PK_ID, 0) will return the PK_ID value if there is one, or return a zero if it is null. This could also be coded with the Value and Coalesce functions. All three would return the same result. The default specified must match the column definition. For example since PK_ID is numeric, then the default must be a numeric. In this case zero.

6) Any SQL statement containing one of the following Aggregate functions should have a Null-Indicator host variable as part of the select (Min, Max, Avg, Sum). DB2 will return a null indicator back to the program if it finds no data to process these functions, requiring the Cobol program to have defined a null indicator. If the program is not set up with a null indicator, an invalid -305 SQLCODE is returned. It is preferable to code the Value, Coalesce, or Ifnull function to alleviate any null indicator logic. For Example:

```
SELECT IFNULL(AVG(SALARY), 0)
FROM EMPLOYEE
WHERE WORKDEPT = 'XYZ'
```

This will either return the average if rows are found, or will return a zero if no rows were met in order to calculate an average.

7) Minimize the number of times cursors are opened and closed during execution. If most of the time the open cursor and fetch only retrieves 1 row, then code a simple Select statement and only execute the cursor processing when a -811 (duplicate rows) is returned.

Do not break up processing into multiple cursors. If it takes a 7-table join, then code all 7 tables in 1 cursor and let DB2 do the work. By breaking it up, the process usually takes longer due to the extra times DB2 is sent SQL statements to process. Only break up the join when all other tuning efforts have been applied. Typically it would be more efficient to execute a 7-table join.

8) Case statements should always contain an ELSE clause. If none of the conditions in the case are met, then DB2 will return a null (via a null indicator) back to the program. If the program is not set up to handle a null being returned from the case statement, then a -305 Sqlcode is returned, usually causing the program to abend.

9) Always display out counts for the number of Selects, Inserts, Updates, Deletes, and Open cursors that have been executed in the program. The overhead in Cobol to define the counters and increment them through the processing is minimal to the overall runtime of the program. This is invaluable information when problems occur in the program that a developer needs to look into. Make sure the counts are displayed out on every abend, and at the end of processing.

10) Always display out the values in host variables for a SQL statement that has an invalid SQL return code and the program goes into its abend error routine. There is nothing more frustrating to a developer than to get a program that errors out or even worse abends, and not knowing what values were being processed.

11) Watch out for any SQL warnings that may occur in an SQL statement. Most programs seem to ignore warnings which many times help to detect potential problems. There are two indications of a warning message in the SQLCA: One is a positive SQLCODE other than +100; the other is a W in the SQLCA's SQLWARN0 field. When either of these exists, DB2 is issuing a warning that something worrisome happened on the prior call and that while you may have received data back, it may not be what you expected. When SQLWARN0 is a W, DB2 also provides helpful information about the problem in one or more of the other SQLWARNn fields. Warnings should also be checked on every SQL statement return. For example:

```
Evaluate SQLCODE
  When 0
    If SQLWARN0 = 'W'
      Display '***  Warning error ***'
      Display Sqlstate = ' Sqlstate
    End-If
  When Other
    .......
End-Evaluate
```

12) Take advantage of the SQLERRD (3) out of the SQLCA. The third occurrence of the SQLERRD array is one of the most useful fields in the SQLCA. This field is populated after a successful insert, update, or delete with a count of the number of rows inserted, updated, or deleted. This is not populated when a mass delete with no 'Where' logic is coded or populated due to deletes affected by delete cascade.

13) Take advantage of fetching rowsets in your cursor processing. See tuning tip #46. This should be strictly enforced for large cursors because of the runtime savings.

ALL SQL PROGRAMS:

1) All SQL join statements are to have the columns from each table noted with a Correlation ID when referenced in Select, Where, Group By, or Order By clauses. A Correlation ID should be something other than a letter of the alphabet. Use something descriptive so others can understand from which table each column is coming from. It makes the join logic more clear and readable.

2) Do not apply any SQL Scalar functions against columns coded in the Where clause. This is especially important for columns that make up any index for a table.

Example 1:

By coding 'Select Integer(CLM_ID') will automatically eliminate the use of the index for CLM_ID.

Example 2:

Where Year(Date_Col1) = 2003 ... should be coded as

Where Date_Col1 between '2003-01-01'
                  and '2003-12-31'

making it an indexable predicate.

3) Check your queries with the DB2 Explain tool. A Plan_Table under your ID will need to be created from the DBAs, or use the Plan_Table defined for theDB2 subsystem you are operating under.

Delete from Plan_Table
;

Explain Plan Set Queryno = 11 for

```
SELECT  CMT_FIRST_NAME,
        CMT_LAST_NAME,
        CMT_SSN,
        CMT_ES_STATUS_CD
 FROM CLAIMANT_CMT
 WHERE CMT_ID = ?


;

Select * from Plan_Table
Order by Queryno, Planno, Qblockno, Mixopseq
;
```

4) Watch out for 'Order By' and 'Group By' statements in queries. Each of these may cause a sort, which requires runtime. Code them only if needed. The fewer columns and rows in any sort will make the sort run faster, so make sure only the columns needed are coded.

5) When coding UNION statements in SQL, start with UNION ALL. By just coding UNION, a sort gets executed to eliminate duplicates, causing more runtime. Many times there never are duplicates, so UNION ALL should be the choice which eliminates a sort taking place.

6) Watch out for DISTINCT. This also causes a sort, which requires more runtime. Only code this when absolutely necessary. Many times, a Group By statement or Subqueries will also get the same result more efficiently. See tuning tip #4.

7) Case statements should always contain an ELSE clause. If none of the conditions in the case logic are met, then DB2 will return a null (via a null indicator) back to the program. If the program is not set up to handle a null, then logic problems could occur, or in the case of Cobol a -305 SQL error.

8) Do not use 'Select Count(*)' for existence checking. Use this only when a total number of rows are needed. Existence checking should be done using the SYSIBM.SYSDUMMY1 table with a correlated subquery using the predicate D1.IBMREQD = D1.IBMREQD. See Existence Checking in Chapter 5.

9) Always check the Summary of Predicate Processing in the DB2 Administration Guide for how to code (or how not to code) predicates to make them indexable and/or Stage 1 versus Stage 2. See tuning tip #14. The DB2 Visual Explain V8 tool will also note any Stage 2 predicates.

10) Watch out for <> (not equal) predicates. These predicates are Non Indexable, but they are Stage 1.

11) Make sure there is an understanding of Inner vs. Outer joins. Many times SQL is written with Table1 Outer Joined to Table2, then Inner joined to Table3. The Inner join being coded last can offset what exceptions took place in the Outer join. Many times the 3 tables could all be coded with Inner joins, which would run more efficiently. Outer joins are not inefficient, but if they bring in extra exception rows, and a subsequent Inner join then gets rid of those extra rows, it was processing not needed.

Also, make sure that if Outer Joins are coded, the program is set up to handle Nulls being returned from the table where the join is not met. This is another area where the Value, Coalesce or Ifnull function should be used to keep DB2 from trying to send a null indicator back to the program.

12) Try to stay away from NOT logic in general. Try to keep predicates positive as much as possible. For example, the following predicate

Where Not Eff_Date > :Ws-Date

could be recoded as

Where Eff_Date <= :Ws-Date

13) When coding predicates, keep the logic away from the column to make it an indexable predicate. For example:

Where Salary * 1.10 > 100000.00

is a non-indexable predicate and should be coded as

Where Salary > 100000.00 / 1.1

14) When using Date Labeled Durations (adding or subtracting years/months/days) to a date, it is logically important in which order they are coded and executed.

For example when adding, the order should be Years first, then Months, then Days.

Select Current Date + 2 years + 3 months + 1 day

When subtracting, the order should be just the opposite. Days first, then Months, then Years:

Select Current Date – 1 days – 3 months – 2 years

This is important, because if they are coded in a different order, the results could be incorrect!

15) If a developer needs to know the last day of a month, there exists a Last_Day SQL function to get it. For Example:

```
Select Last_Day(Current Date)
Into :HV1      -- Where HV1 is some Host Variable
From Sysibm.Sysdummy1
```

16) A more efficient way to get the same result is to use the Set SQL Set statement. For example:

```
Set :HV1 = Last_Day(Current Date)
```

NOTE: Use the 'Set Host Variable' Assignment over the SYSIBM.SYSDUMMY1 whenever possible, especially when the statement may get executed hundreds or thousands of times within its runtime.

17) Take advantage of the many Date functions in SQL instead of programming code to provide the information needed.

Year/Month/Day – Returns only that portion of the date value

DayofWeek / DayofWeek_Iso – Returns a number (1-7), depending if the week begins on Sunday or Monday.

DayofMonth / DayofYear – Returns the specific day number. Month (1-31). Year (1-365).

Last_Day – Returns the last day of the month for a specific date. If the date was 01/15/2005, the date returned would be 10/31/2005.

Next_Day – Returns the next day's date for a specific date. If the date was 01/31/2005, the date returned would be 02/01/2005.

Days – Used to get the days difference between 2 dates.

   Select Days(Hiredate) – Days(Birthdate)

   returns the number of days difference.

Date functions cont…

Week – Returns a number (1-53) that represents the week of the year. Week 1 is the first week that contains the first day of the year.

Week_Iso – Returns a number (1-53) that represents the week of the year. Week 1 is the first week that contains a Thursday.

Char – Used to get a date column back in a specific format (USA, ISO or JIS, EUR).

CHAPTER 4: SQL PROGRAM WALKTHROUGHS

Program walkthroughs are one of the most crucial tasks in getting applications ready for production. As was stated at the beginning of this book there are a lot of SQL developers in shops worldwide, but many do not know of or think about some of the coding consequences that need to be reviewed and pointed out. By reviewing code and checking/asking for the following points, it is certain that applications will perform better and have drastically fewer defects and incidents bneing reported in production.

Management typically states that there is no time for walkthroughs. But a quick 15 minute check through the list in this chapter can alleviate so many potential problems. I personally find it hard to believe that management in many shops do not understand the consequences of poor program design or poor SQL coding that can make programs run hours versus minutes, or minutes versus seconds. Walkthroughs are teachable training moments that will only make the development staff stronger in future efforts. And it is not only about performance. Reviewing program code can alleviate production issues that could arise sometime after the program is promoted back to production. Developers get blamed for many productions issues, but I think management also has to take blame for not having in place 15 minute walkthrough procedures that can minimize issues from occurring in production.

1) **Have all programmers bring the following to each review.**
   - A copy of their latest compiled code
   - A copy of the latest DB2 Explain
   - A copy of the latest execution. From this we want to see the CPU time, Actual time of execution, control counts (# Open Cursors, # Inserts, # Deletes, # Random Selects, # Rows Fetched, # Stored Procedure Calls, etc)

2) **Evaluate each SQL statement in the DB2 Explain.**
   - Check for any Tablespace scans
   - Check for any Index Scans (Index usage with 0 matching columns)
   - Check for any Sorts taking place. Are they needed? Is there another way to code the query to eliminate the sorts?
   - Check the Join Methods, and any associated Sorts specific to that join method

3) **Evaluate each of the SQL statements in the code.**

   - Should any Inner joins be coded as Outer joins? Understand the relationships between all tables in each join. Ensure that the developer understands the relationships and has coded the correct join.
   - Should any Outer join be coded as an Inner join?
   - Check all Union SQL statements. Do they need to code Union or can the SQL statement be Union All?

Evaluate each of the SQL statements cont...

- Check all columns in each query. Are any of them nullable columns? Is the SQL coded to handle a null value if no actual value exists for some rows? This will eliminate any –305 SQL abends.
- Does each SQL statement need all the columns being selected?
- For every AVG, MIN, MAX, or SUM statement, make sure the SQL is coded to handle a null value. This will eliminate any -305 SQL abends.
- Check all Order By statements. Are they needed?
- Check all Distinct statements. Can there definitely be duplicates? Can it be coded with a Group By, or rewritten as a Correlated or Non-Correlated subquery?
- Check all CASE statements. Ensure that an 'Else' is coded to cover any of the conditions that are not met. This will eliminate -305 SQL abends.
- Check every predicate to make sure that there are no Scalar Functions against any of the columns. Make sure all mathematics is done on the opposite side of the operator and not against the column itself.
- Look for any 'Not' logic. Many times there is a positive way to code the predicate which typically makes it more efficient. Most all predicates containing 'Not' logic are non indexable and Stage 2.

Evaluate each of the SQL statements cont...

- For readability and understandability, make sure all joins and correlated subqueries have correlation IDs in them. Make sure the correlation IDs are coded not just in the join predicates, but also in the Select, Order By, Group By, etc. Do not code correlation IDs of A, B, C, and D values, rather make them something meaningful to help the SQL statement more readable.
- Code each predicate on a separate line.
- Code each table in a multi table join on a separate line.
- Code proper indents and generally make the SQL neat and readable. There exists SQL formatting websites to help in the formatting if the queries become too involved.

4). Evaluate the overall program logic:

- Are there other ways to get final results any faster? Many times developers do not see alternative ways to process through the data in order to build their report or result sets. Program walkthroughs are the perfect time to review other ideas.

In batch programs where most of the data is being processed:

- Can we minimize any I/O going on?
- Can we reduce any CPU usage?
- Can we cut back on the number of times SQL requests are being passed to the database manager?
- Can we take advantage of (or build) any Summary or Global Temporary tables to help the process and minimize I/O taking place?

5). Check for programming standards being followed.

Programming standards are written for many reasons. Some of the more common reasons are readability, efficiency, and to minimize production incident reporting. If you let all developers code the way they are most comfortable with, then more problems occur. Make sure all developers know of any programming standards, but most importantly make sure someone performs some kind of quality assurance before the code ever gets promoted to production to ensure standards are being followed.

CHAPTER 5: EXISTENCE CHECKING

There are many queries in programs that execute SQL 'Select Count(*)' statements just to see if any rows exist for particular data. Many times it doesn't matter whether there is one row or one million rows, only if any rows exist. When this is the case, 'Select Count(*)' is the most expensive way to check because it will count up all rows. Queries should be coded so they ensure stopping after getting a hit on the first row unless of course they actually need the total number of rows. There are other ways to code existence checking that are also not very efficient, and this chapter lays some of these out, with the more efficient rewrites.

Example 1:

```
EXEC SQL
    SELECT        COUNT(*)
    INTO :HOST-VARIABLE1
    FROM   TABLE1
    WHERE  COLUMN1   = :HOST-VARIABLE-X
       AND COLUMN2   = :HOST-VARIABLE-Y
END-EXEC

IF  HOST-VARIABLE1 > ZERO
  SET ROWS-FOUND  TO TRUE
END-IF
```

NOTE: HOST-VARIABLE1 will contain the total number of rows that meet the criteria.

Existence Checking cont...

The better way to code this is using the SYSIBM.SYSDUMMY1 table which only contains 1 row with 1 column. It is a dummy table that is part of the DB2 system and gets used for many different purposes in SQL. Coding the join statement D1.IBMREQD = D1.IBMREQD in the following subquery (making it a correlated subquery) ensures that the Exist Subquery will stop after it hits the first row that meets the criteria. This can save hundreds or thousands of DB2 Getpage requests, which ultimately reduces runtime.

```
MOVE ZEROS TO HOST_VRIABLE1

SELECT  1
INTO   :HOST-VARIABLE1
FROM SYSIBM.SYSDUMMY1 D1
WHERE EXISTS
     (SELECT 1
      FROM   TABLE1
      WHERE  COLUMN1  = :HOST-VARIABLE-X
        AND  COLUMN2  = :HOST-VARIABLE-Y
        AND  D1.IBMREQD = D1.IBMREQD)

EVALUATE SQLCODE .....

IF  HOST-VARIABLE1  >  ZERO
  SET  ROWS-FOUND  TO TRUE
  END-IF
```

continued...

Existence Checking cont...

As of DB2 V7, the following SQL will also perform as efficiently, and is a more straight forward coding style.

```
SELECT  1
INTO   :HOST-VARIABLE1
FROM   TABLE1
WHERE  COLUMN1   = :HOST-VARIABLE-X
   AND  COLUMN2   = :HOST-VARIABLE-Y
FETCH FIRST 1 ROW ONLY

EVALUATE SQLCODE .....

IF   HOST-VARIABLE1  >  ZERO
   SET  ROWS-FOUND   TO TRUE
END-IF
```

There are many Exists queries that get checked for existence with a non correlated subquery. This is very inefficient because the subquery will still go through all rows that meet the criteria before noting that there is existence or not. For existence checking only, the subquery should be coded as a correlated subquery in order to have the processing stop at the first row that meets the criteria.

continued...

Existence Checking cont...

Example 2:

```
SELECT 1
INTO :HOST-VARIABLE1
FROM SYSIBM.SYSDUMMY1
WHERE EXISTS
 (SELECT 1
  FROM   TABLE1
  WHERE  COLUMN1   = :HOST-VARIABLE-X
    AND  COLUMN2   = :HOST-VARIABLE-Y)
```

Should be recoded as:

```
SELECT 1
INTO :HOST-VARIABLE1
FROM SYSIBM.SYSDUMMY1 D1
WHERE EXISTS
 (SELECT 1
  FROM   TABLE1
  WHERE  COLUMN1   = :HOST-VARIABLE-X
    AND  COLUMN2   = :HOST-VARIABLE-Y
    AND  D1.IBMREQD = D1.IBMREQD)
```

CHAPTER 6: RUNSTATS

The major causes of SQL performance problems often times revolve around insufficient statistics on the tables involved. One great thing with DB2 V8 is the ability to run both cardinality and frequency value statistics on both indexed and non indexed columns. This gives the optimizer more information on predicates coded against these columns, making it predict filter factors more accurately. Prior to V8 these statistics could only be run on columns that were part of an index.

When it comes to multi table joins, often times there is a wrong choice by the optimizer on which table is the leading (composite) table. DB2 should choose the table which gets filtered the most, but if insufficient statistics exist on columns of the predicates, DB2 may choose the wrong starting table which typically leads to extra I/O.

Insufficient statistics can also lead the optimizer to make the wrong choice on indexes and/or join methods between the tables. When it comes to single table access, the optimizer may force an incorrect index choice, or no index choice.

continued...

Runstats cont...

In order to stay proactive, especially now that in 2009 most shops are on DB2 V8, IT shops should do the following:

1) All tables should have cardinality statistics for every column in the table.

2) Any table that contains column(s) that have a very skewed (uneven) data distribution should have frequency value statistics on those columns. For example the SEX column in the EMPOYEE table contains 2 values ('M' and 'F'). If one of these values has a high or low percentage of rows affected, then frequency value statistics should be run on this column. Without the frequency value statistics, DB2 assumes even distribution (50% 'M', 50% 'F').

3) Any table that contains column(s) that have a default value which affects many rows should have frequency value statistics on that column. For example the COMM and BONUS columns in the EMPLOYEE table both default to 0. If a high percentage of rows contain 0, then DB2 should know this by running frequency value statistics on these columns.

continued...

Runstats cont...

4) For any SQL queries that contain predicates on columns with frequency value statistics, it is imperative for DB2 to know what value is being processed. The only way for DB2 to know this is to either hard code the value being processed, or for Cobol programs bind with the REOPT parameter. For Java programs, they should wait and do the SQL Prepare after moving the values to their respective host variables.

Typically Java programs execute their SQL Prepare statement when it contains parameter markers. But for special columns with skewed data distributions, the SQL Prepare should happen after the values are received and moved to their variables. See tuning tip #28.

In order to know what frequency value statistics have been run on columns in a table, refer to the SYSIBM.SYSCOLDIST catalog table. The DB2 V8 Visual Explain tool will also show those statistics.

Runstat Guidelines: The RUNSTATS utility should be run:

- When a table is loaded
- When an index is created
- When a tablespace is reorganized
- When there have been extensive updates, deletions, or insertions in a tablespace
- After the recover of a tablespace to a prior point in time

CHAPTER 7:   TEN STEPS TO TUNING A QUERY

Developers often have a program or SQL statement that should be running faster and are not sure exactly where to start. Following is a list of items they should follow in order to find the issue that can improve the performance.

1) Check the predicates. If it is one query, or multiple queries in a program, check every predicate in every query to ensure that they are written as indexable, Stage 1, and as simple and straightforward as possible.

2) If there is a Distinct in the query, take it out and make it a Group By statement. This does not change the logic, but will allow DB2 to still get rid of the duplicate rows without sometimes executing a sort. This will change in DB2 V9 where the Distinct will be looked at the same way as a Group By and look to rid duplicates without sorting if possible. You may also be able to rewrite some of the joins that are causing the duplicates as Exists subqueries. See tuning tip #4.

3) Execute an Explain. From the Explain output check the following:
- Are there any tablespace scans occurring? If so go through the checklist in tuning tip #59 to figure out why.

- Are there any sorts occurring? If the query has a Union, Distinct, Group By or Order By in it, does any of them need to be there?

continued...

Ten Steps continued, executing an Explain

- If there is a join involved, what is the order of tables being processed? DB2 should be selecting the table that will be filtered the most as the starting table. If it is not selecting the table being filtered the most, then check the columns of the predicates and make sure there are enough statistics on these columns to help the optimizer. See tuning tip #12, also Chapter 2. To know which table is going to be filtered the most, the developer must know the values coming in at runtime. They can then execute 'Select count(*)' statements to figure this out.

- All correlated subqueries should use an index, and if possible process with indexonly = yes. See tuning tip #17. Correlated subqueries are subqueries containing a join to a column from the outer table.

- Any Nested Loop Join operations should have their tables being processed using an index with matching columns. If it is the starting (composite) table showing a tablespace scan, then this may not be much of an issue due to the fact that it will only be scanned one time. But for the joined tables, any tablespace scans will causes that table to be scanned numerous times.

continued…

Ten Steps cont...

4) Look at the DB2 statistics for each table and every column involved in the predicates. Make sure the statistics are up to date, and any columns that have skewed (uneven) distribution should have frequency value statistics on these columns. Statistics can be seen in the following DB2 catalog tables (SYSTABLES, SYSCOLUMNS, SYSCOLDIST, SYSINDEXES).

For partitioned tables, statistics exists at each partition in (SYSTABSTATS, SYSCOLSTATS, SYSCOLDISTSTATS, SYSINDEXSTATS).

5) For any columns involved where frequency value statistics are involved, DB2 needs to know of these values and typically does not know based on a host variable at bind or prepare time. See tuning tip #10.

- For Cobol programs, this will require either hardcoding the value for that predicate in the code, or rebinding the program using a REOPT parameter (see tuning tip #51).

- For programs that execute SQL prepare statements, they need to be changed to execute the prepare after the values have been moved to the host variables. This allows DB2 to now see the value for the column that had skewed data at optimization time, and determine based on the frequency value statistics exactly the percentage of rows affected by that predicate. This provides better information to the optimizer whereby it can make better choices in creating its access path.

Ten Steps cont...

6) Check any indexes that have been chosen. Are there any other possible indexes that DB2 could use based on all the predicates? When processing the index, is it matching on any columns? This can be seen in the DB2 Explain tool.

7) Are there any subquery predicates? Change any 'In' subquery to an 'Exists' subquery or vice versa to see if that possibly helps. If there is more than one subquery in the SQL statement, have the most restrictive subquery coded first. See tuning tip #16.

8) Check the number of times SQL statements are being executed in the program. Is there any way to reduce the number of open cursors, selects, etc.? See tuning tip #11

9) Try 'Optimize for 1 Row' at the end of the query. See Chapter 2, item #1. This will not change the logic, but may change the optimization path chosen.

10) Try A.PKEY = A.PKEY, where the 'A' table is the table that you think should be the starting (composite) table. See Chapter 2, item #2.

APPENDIX A. PREDICATE REWRITE EXAMPLES:

Following are some examples of predicates that could be re-written to be more efficient, more simple, more readable, and understandable. These predicates are stage 2 as of DB2 V8, and could possibly change in upcoming version releases. Sometimes developers have predicates and are not sure exactly how to rewrite them. These examples can give them a start. Remember that when coding the 'Between' predicate, the values being checked are inclusive. With the 'Not Between' predicate, the values are not inclusive. Also when coding 'Between' and 'Not Between' predicates, it is logically important to list the lower value first.

Stage 2	Stage 1
1) WHERE YEAR(HIREDATE) = 1980	WHERE HIREDATE BETWEEN '1980-01-01' AND '1980-12-31'
2) WHERE '2000-01-01' BETWEEN DATE_COL1 AND DATE_COL2	WHERE DATE_COL1 <= '2000-01-01' AND DATE_COL2 >= '2000-01-01'
3) WHERE '2000-01-01' NOT BETWEEN DATE_COL1 AND DATE_COL2	WHERE DATE_COL1 > '2000-01-01' OR DATE_COL2 < '2000-01-01'

NOTE: ** DATE_COL1 MUST BE THE LOWER OF THE VALUES BETWEEN THE 2 DATE COLUMNS **

4) WHERE DIGITS(EDLEVEL) = :HV3	WHERE EDLEVEL = SMALLINT(:HV3)

NOTE: ** SMALLINT MATCHES THE DEFINITION OF EDLEVEL **

5) WHERE HIREDATE NOT BETWEEN '1985-01-01' AND '1985-12-31'	WHERE HIREDATE < '1985-01-01' OR HIREDATE > '1985-01-01'

continued…

168

Stage 2	Stage 1
5) WHERE HIREDATE NOT BETWEEN '1985-01-01' AND '1985-12-31'	WHERE HIREDATE < '1985-01-01' OR HIREDATE > '1985-01-01'
6) WHERE HIREDATE + 7 DAYS > :HV-DATE)	WHERE HIREDATE > DATE(:HV-DATE) – 7 DAYS
7) WHERE SALARY * 1.1 > 60000.00	WHERE SALARY > 60000.00 / 1.1
8) WHERE HIREDATE + 1 MONTH > :HV-DATE	WHERE HIREDATE > DATE(:HV-DATE) – 1 MONTH
9) WHERE EMPNO = (SELECT MAX(EMPNO) FROM EMP WHERE ...)	**IF EMPNO IS DEFINED AS 'NOT NULL'** WHERE EMPNO = (SELECT COALESCE(MAX(EMPNO),0) FROM EMP WHERE ...)
10) WHERE SUBSTR(DEPTNO,1,1) = 'A'	WHERE DEPTNO LIKE 'A%'
11) SELECT DISTINCT E.EMPNO, E.LASTNAME FROM EMP E, EMPPROJACT EP WHERE E.EMPNO = EP.EMPNO AND ...	SELECT E.EMPNO, E.LASTNAME FROM EMP E, EMPPROJACT EP WHERE E.EMPNO = EP.EMPNO AND ... GROUP BY E.EMPNO, E.LASTNAME
12) WHERE D.DEPTNO > :HV-DEPTNO AND (D.LOC = :HV-LOC OR D.ADMRDEPT = :HV-ADMRDEPT)	WHERE (D.DEPTNO > :HV-DEPTNO AND D.LOC = :HV-LOC) OR (D.DEPTNO > :HV-DEPTNO AND D.ADMRDEPT = :HV-ADMRDEPT)
13) WHERE BONUS = :HV1 + :HV2	COMPUTE HV3 = HV1 + HV2 SELECT ... FROM ... WHERE BONUS = :HV3 OR WHERE BONUS = DEC(:HV1 + :HV2, 9,2)

NOTE: ** THIS ENSURES THE ADDITION IS FORMATTED
** EXACTLY AS HOW BONUS IS DEFINED DEC(9,2)

continued...

Stage 2

Stage 1

14) SELECT D.DEPTNO, D.DEPTNAME
    FROM DEPARTMENT D LEFT JOIN
        EMPLOYEE   E
        ON D.DEPTNO = E.WORKDEPT
    WHERE E.WORKDEPT IS NOT NULL

SELECT D.DEPTNO, D.DEPTNAME
    FROM DEPARTMENT D
    WHERE NOT EXISTS
      (SELECT 1
       FROM EMPLOYEE E
       WHERE D.DEPTNO = E.WORKDEPT)

NOTE: ** THIS QUERY FILTERS AFTER
THE JOIN. A PREDICATE THAT IS
EVALUATED AFTER A JOIN OPERATION
IS ALWAYS A STAGE 2 PREDICATE.

** THIS QUERY FILTERS DURING
   THE JOIN

APPENDIX B. TERMINOLOGY

Every DB2 application requires three components to operate: the system, the database and the application itself. The system refers to the DB2 subsystem installation. The database refers to the database objects that house the application data, and the application is the host language and SQL code that process the data for the users. To effectively deliver good DB2 performance, system programmers, database analysts, and developers must be able to monitor and tune each of these components.

Cardinality: Cardinality usually refers to a column and the number of distinct values for that column across all rows of data in a table. For example the EMPLOYEE table has 42 rows where there are 42 different values for the column EMPNO. EMPNO is said to have high cardinality. The column SEX has 2 values, and is said to have low cardinality

Clustering index: This is the index that determines how rows are physically ordered (clustered) in a table space. If a clustering index on a partitioned table is not a partitioning index, the rows are ordered in cluster sequence within each data partition instead of spanning the partitions. Prior to Version 8 of DB2 Universal Database™ for z/OS, the partitioning index was required to be the clustering index.

DB2 Subsystem performance and tuning consists of managing memory (Buffer Pools, EDM Pools, RID Pools, Sort Pools, etc.), DASD storage management, proper usage of database logs, managing operating system resources, configuring locking system parameters, managing DB2 data-sharing, to name a few.

DB2 Database Objects consists of tablespaces, tables, and indexes that comprise a database application. A huge factor for ensuring efficient data base objects is database design. This typically means having a fully normalized logical data model for every application.

After data is initially loaded, it is important to run statistics from time to time on the database objects so DB2 knows more about the data distributions in the structures.

Inaccurate, outdated, or missing statistics are one of the leading causes for poor performance in applications. Statistics are accumulated and loaded via the DB2 Runstats utility. Another cause of poor performance can be mis-managing the tablespace files that house the files. These files are physical structures that need to be sized for initial loads and growth. The physical breaking out into extents or fragmentation, or even worse running out of space, will all cause performance issues.

DB2 Application Performance consists of 2 parts: Application host language code and SQL code embedded into the application programs. Many languages are fairly easy to learn, including SQL, but not quite so easy to master or to fully understand many of their inadequacies that have an impact on performance. This book hits on most of the performance inefficiencies of the SQL language.

FILTER FACTOR: For every predicate in every query, DB2 will determine what is called a filter factor. It is an estimate from DB2 on the percentage of rows it thinks will be affected by that predicate. For example the employee table has 42 rows where the EMPNO column is the primary key. Predicate = WHERE EMPNO = :HV-EMPNO, DB2 will estimate 1/42 = .02381 percent of the data will be affected by this predicate. Total rows affected = 42 * .02381 = 1. The filter factor for this predicate = .02381. Predicate = WHERE WORKDEPT = :HV-DEPTNO, DB2 will estimate a filter factor of 1/8 = .125 because it knows based on cardinality statistics that there are 8 different values out of the 42 total rows for column = DEPTNO. Total rows affected = 42 * .125 = 5.25.

FREQUENCY VALUE STATISTICS: Besides cardinality statistics, another kind of Runstat statistic is called frequency value. This type of statistic list by specific values the percentage of rows affected a table. For example if frequency value statistics were run against the column WORKDEPT in the EMPLOYEE table, DB2 would know the following for the 8 different values. Value 'A00' affects 5 rows. 5/42 = .12 percent of the data 'D11' affects 11 rows. 11/42 = .26 percent of the data etc...

So, if predicate = WHERE WORKDEPT = :HV-DEPTNO, DB2 thinks the filter factor = .125 but if predicate = WHERE WORKDEPT = 'D11', DB2 knows the exact filter factor = .26.

Frequency value statistics are great for the optimizer because it can then know for sure the exact number of affected rows, but only if it knows the value at bind or prepare time. In order to do this the value would either have to be hard coded, or a 'REOPT' parameter would be needed in the bind process so another optimization takes place during runtime when the value is placed in the host variable.

Indexable Predicate: A predicate that is written in such a way as to allow the optimizer the opportunity to match index entries on the column in the predicate, if an index exists. For example the following predicates are non-indexable, meaning that even if there is an index on the column = HIREDATE, no matching index processing will take place. The index may possibly be chosen to process, but it would be an index scan with 0 matching columns.

> **WHERE HIREDATE <> '1985-01-01'**
> **OR WHERE YEAR(HIREDATE) = 1985**
> **OR WHERE HIREDATE – 1 MONTH < :HV-DATE**

Join Methods: For OS/390 and Z/Os DB2 systems, there are 3 different join types that DB2 can choose from in order to process the I/O between tables involved in a join:

Nested Loop Join. To perform a Nested Loop Join, a qualifying row is identified in the outer table, and then the inner table is scanned searching for a match. A qualifying row is one in which the predicates for columns in the table match. When the inner table scan is complete, another qualifying row in the outer table is identified.

The inner table is scanned for a match again, and so on. The repeated scanning of the inner table is hopefully accomplished with an index, or the inner table gets scanned numerous times causing long runtimes.

Merge Scan Join. With the MJ, the tables to be joined need to be ordered by the join predicates. That means that each table must be accessed in order by the columns that specify the join criteria. This ordering can be the result of either a sort or indexed access. After ensuring that both the outer and inner tables are properly sequenced, each table is read sequentially, and the join columns are matched up. Neither table is read more than once during a merge scan join. The ordering takes place after all qualifying rows have been selected.

Hybrid Join: The hybrid join combines data and pointers to access and combine the rows from the tables being joined.

In general, the nested loop join is preferred in terms of execution cost when a small number of rows qualify for the starting composite table. As the number of qualifying rows increases, the merge join becomes a better choice.

Inner join: The result of a join operation that includes only the matched rows of both tables that are being joined.

Outer join: The result of a join operation that includes the matched rows of both tables and the unmatched rows of the table being joined to. These unmatched rows are called the exceptions, and the outer join preserves these rows even though a match is not found on the joined table. Any columns being returned from the joined table will be sent back as nulls.

Reoptimization: The process of reconsidering, at run time, the access path of an SQL statement that has already been optimized at bind or prepare time. During reoptimization, the actual values of host variables, parameter markers, and special registers might be considered in choosing the access path.

Stage 1 Predicates: Evaluated at the time data rows are retrieved (sargable). There is big performance gains in having stage 1 predicates because fewer rows are passed to stage 2, minimizing I/O and reducing processor time. Sargeable is an old RDMS term meaning 'Searchable Argument'.

Stage 2 Predicates: Evaluated after data retrieval (non sargable) which is more expensive than stage 1. Stage 2 handles sort issues and optimizer duties and is responsible for applying and checking the more involved and intricate predicates. It also applies to character concatenation, most scalar functions, data conversion, and arithmetic expressions.

Visual Explain: This is a great tool for any DB2 SQL developer that can be used to detail the access paths chosen by the DB2 optimizer. It is another form of the DB2 Explain tool that graphically lays out the access paths. The information provided is invaluable for resolving many types of performance issues with a program or query. It provides all the details of a regular DB2 Explain that uses the Plan_Table and DSN_Statemnt_Table, along with statistics, predicate types, and more.

continued...

Visual Explain cont...

Some of the information Visual Explain provides:

- Order of tables to process
- Whether indexes have been chosen
- Any sorts taking place
- The reason for any sorts
- Join Types between tables
- Stage 1 and Stage predicates
- Matching index predicates versus index screening
  predicates
- Generated filter factors for every predicate
- Generated overall filter factor
- All cardinality statistics
- All frequency value statistics
- All indexes on tables involved
- Table and column statistics
- Any materialized work file tables